COURSE 1

McDougal Littell Middle School

Math

Larson   Boswell   Kanold   Stiff

CHAPTER 7

Resource Book

The Resource Book contains a wide variety of blackline masters available for Chapter 7. The blacklines are organized by lesson. Included are support materials for the teacher as well as practice, activities, applications, and project resources.

McDougal Littell
A HOUGHTON MIFFLIN COMPANY
Evanston, Illinois • Boston • Dallas

Contributing Authors

The authors wish to thank the following individuals for their contributions to the Chapter 7 Resource Book.

Donna Foley

Rebecca Salmon Glus

Julie Groth

Mark Johnson

Patrick M. Kelly

Leslie Palmer

Jessica Pflueger

Barbara L. Power

Monica Single

ISBN: 0-618-26090-0

23456789–MDO–07 06 05 04 03

Contents

7 Multiplication and Division of Fractions

Contents

Contents

Descriptions of Resources

This Chapter Resource Book is organized by lessons within the chapter in order to make your planning easier. The following materials are provided:

Tips for New Teachers   These teaching notes provide both new and experienced teachers with useful teaching tips for each lesson, including tips about common errors and inclusion.

Parents as Partners   This guide helps parents contribute to student success by providing an overview of the chapter along with questions and activities for parents and students to work on together.

Lesson Plans and Lesson Plans for Block Scheduling   This planning template helps teachers select the materials they will use to teach each lesson from among the variety of materials available for the lesson. The block-scheduling version provides additional information about pacing.

Activity Support Masters   These blackline masters make it easier for students to record their work on selected activities in the Student Edition.

Technology Activities with Keystrokes   Keystrokes for various models of calculators are provided for each Technology Activity in the Student Edition where appropriate, along with alternative Technology Activities for selected lessons.

Practice A, B, and C   These exercises offer additional practice for the material in each lesson, including application problems. There are three levels of practice for each lesson: A (basic), B (average), and C (advanced).

Study Guide   These two pages provide additional instruction, worked-out examples, and practice exercises covering the key concepts and vocabulary in each lesson.

Real-World Problem Solving   These exercises offer problem-solving activities for the material in each lesson in a real world context.

Challenge Practice   These exercises offer challenging practice on the mathematics of each lesson for advanced students.

Chapter Review Games and Activities   This worksheet offers fun practice at the end of the chapter and provides an alternative way to review the chapter content in preparation for the Chapter Test.

Projects with Rubric   These projects allow students to delve more deeply into a problem that applies the mathematics of the chapter. Teacher's notes and a 4-point rubric are included. The projects include a real-life project, a cooperative project, and an independent extra credit project.

Cumulative Practice   These practice pages help students maintain skills from the current chapter and preceding chapters.

Tips for New Teachers

For use with Chapter 7

Lesson 7.1

TEACHING TIP   Continue the use of concrete models before moving on to the abstract concept of multiplying a fraction by a whole number. Provide numerous examples such as the following (refer to the diagram below): Have students each take a sheet of $\frac{1}{2}$ inch grid paper and draw a border around 3 separate rows of five units. Have them shade in $\frac{3}{5}$ of each of the 3 rows, representing the multiplication problem, $3 \times \frac{3}{5}$. Ask students to find the sum of the shaded units $\left(\frac{9}{5}\right)$. Check for understanding, particularly for students who incorrectly answer $\frac{9}{15}$. Remind students that the size of each unit has not changed; each unit is still $\frac{1}{5}$ in size. So, the answer must be $\frac{9}{5}$. Finally, connect this concrete model to multiplication. Remind students that multiplication is a simplified way to perform multiple additions. Repeat this process with other concrete models until you are confident that your students have a good grasp of the concept.

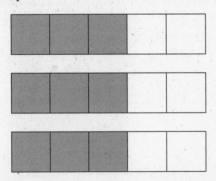

COMMON ERROR   Be sure students understand that when you multiply a whole number greater than 1 by a fraction less than 1, the product is less than the whole number and greater than the fraction. Note that in the above Teaching Tip, $\frac{9}{15} = \frac{3}{5}$, and therefore could not possibly be the correct answer.

TEACHING TIP   Be sure to assign Exercise 35 on page 316 and use it as an opportunity to reinforce the concept that the sum of all the fractional parts of a circle graph must always equal one.

Hands-on Activity 7.2

TEACHING TIP   As you complete this activity, ask students to look at the product of two fractions that are less than 1. Have students compare the product to each of the fractions. See if they realize that the product is less than both of the fractions. Ask them if they think this will always be true.

Lesson 7.2

COMMON ERROR   After completing the 7.2 Hands-on Activity, point out to students that at no time did they have to find a least common denominator. Reinforce that only the operations of addition and subtraction of fractions require finding the LCD.

TEACHING TIP   Starting with Example 4, when students simplify before multiplying, stress the importance of neatness in crossing out the original factor and clearly writing the remaining factor. Encourage students to skip at least one line between problems on their papers.

COMMON ERROR   Students may not fully understand the concept of simplifying before multiplying and may simplify incorrectly. Reinforce that simplifying requires that they divide one number in the numerator and one number in the denominator by the same factor. For example, in $\frac{3}{5} \times \frac{1}{10}$, the 5 and 10 cannot be simplified as a pair. Likewise, in $\frac{2}{3} \times \frac{1}{4} \times \frac{5}{6}$, the 2 can be paired with only the 4 or the 6, but not both.

Lesson 7.3

TEACHING TIP   The process of multiplying mixed numbers requires many steps and, thus, contains many places for students to make errors. You will want students to show all their steps so that you can more easily detect and remedy any errors they make.

TEACHING TIP   Remind students to write mixed numbers in fraction form before attempting to simplify.

Tips for New Teachers

For use with Chapter 7

Hands-on Activity 7.4

TEACHING TIP Supply students with rulers that are only marked in increments of $\frac{1}{8}$ inch since any extra lines will likely confuse students during this activity.

TEACHING TIP You may wish to extend the table in Exercise 2 to include $1\frac{1}{2}$ and $2\frac{1}{4}$ as dividends since they are also compatible with $\frac{3}{8}$. This way you can introduce division involving mixed numbers.

COMMON ERROR Students may develop a false sense that all quotients will be whole numbers. You might wish to explain that these examples were specifically chosen to help students develop a pattern and that not all quotients will be whole numbers.

Lesson 7.4

COMMON ERROR Reinforce to students that they will take the reciprocal of the divisor only. You may wish to point out to students that the dividend is the starting point and that the starting point cannot change.

TEACHING TIP Remind students that a whole number can be written as a fraction with a denominator of one. This will help them to correctly find reciprocals of whole numbers.

Lesson 7.5

TEACHING TIP Students may again experience the same difficulties as in multiplying mixed numbers due to the many steps required to find the answer. Reinforce the need to show all steps and to show them neatly.

Lesson 7.6

TEACHING TIP Students need real-life examples of relative weights and capacities. You may wish to bring in items that weigh approximately one ounce or one pound. Have scales or balances set up in the classroom for students to weigh these items. This will give students a foundation of what an ounce and a pound actually are. For capacity, you may wish to bring in measuring cups of various sizes. You can bring in a bag of rice and a bag of sand to show that a cup of each will have the same capacity but different weights.

COMMON ERROR Students tend to confuse ounce and fluid ounce. Remind them that ounce is a unit of *weight* and that fluid ounce is a unit of *capacity*.

Lesson 7.7

TEACHING TIP Students frequently are confused as to whether to multiply or divide when changing units of measure. Remind them that one will need more of a smaller unit. Thus, one would multiply to change from a larger unit to a smaller unit. Likewise, one will need less of a larger unit. Thus, one would divide to change from a smaller unit to a larger unit.

Name _____ Date _____

Parents as Partners

For use with Chapter 7

Chapter Overview One way you can help your student succeed in Chapter 7 is by discussing the lesson goals in the chart below. When a lesson is completed, ask your student the following questions. "What were the goals of the lesson? What new words and formulas did you learn? How can you apply the ideas of the lesson to your life?"

Lesson Title	Lesson Goals	Key Applications
7.1: Multiplying Fractions and Whole Numbers	Multiplying fractions and whole numbers. Use mental math or a model. Estimate a product.	• Party Music • CD Rack • National Parks • Travel Postcards
7.2: Multiplying Fractions	Multiply fractions.	• Scooter Sales • Soap Bubbles • Fingernails • Glaciers
7.3: Multiplying Mixed Numbers	Multiply mixed numbers.	• Trampoline • Soccer • Geometry
7.4: Dividing Fractions	Write reciprocals. Use reciprocals to divide fractions.	• Caves • Magnets • Clay Cups and Mugs
7.5: Dividing Mixed Numbers	Divide mixed numbers. Choose an operation by thinking of a similar problem.	• Cider • Volunteer Work • Alligators • Talent Show
7.6: Weight and Capacity in Customary Units	Use customary units of weight and capacity.	• Bakery • Animals • Hang Glider
7.7: Changing Customary Units	Change customary units of measure. Multiply by a form of 1. Find a relationship. Add and subtract measurements.	• Camels • Model Trains • Maple Syrup • Submersibles

Know How to Take Notes

Drawing a Model is the strategy featured in Chapter 7 (see page 312). Encourage your student to draw any visual models (pictures, graphs, charts, etc.) that are used in the lesson. Your student could also include his/her own original visual models to help remember a difficult concept or example. Have your student explain what each model represents and how it does this. To be most beneficial, students need to be as accurate and detailed as possible when drawing a model.

Name _____ Date _____

Parents as Partners

For use with Chapter 7

Key Ideas Your student can demonstrate understanding of key concepts by working through the following exercises with you.

Lesson	Exercise
7.1	You spend $\frac{3}{4}$ hour each day practicing the piano. How many hours are spent practicing each week? each month (30 days)?
7.2	$\frac{7}{8}$ of the students from a school participated in the school's Winter Carnival. $\frac{2}{3}$ of the students who participated in the carnival won prizes. What fraction of the total number of students won prizes? Bonus: If there are 600 students in the school, how many students won prizes?
7.3	You attend school from 8:30 A.M. to 3:20 P.M. How many hours is this? Write your answer as a mixed number. Of those hours, you are in class $\frac{3}{4}$ of the time. How many hours are you in class?
7.4	Your cat weighs 4 kilograms. Your gerbil weighs $\frac{3}{10}$ kilogram. How many gerbils would it take to equal the weight of your cat?
7.5	Find the quotient. (a) $3\frac{3}{8} \div \frac{3}{4}$ (b) $\frac{7}{10} \div 4\frac{1}{5}$ (c) $6 \div 6\frac{2}{7}$ (d) $4\frac{5}{6} \div 4\frac{2}{9}$
7.6	Choose an appropriate customary unit to measure the item. (a) capacity of a glass of milk (b) weight of a lunch tray (with lunch on it) (c) capacity of a wading pool (d) weight of a light bulb
7.7	Change the measurement to the specified unit. (a) New curtains require $6\frac{1}{2}$ yards of material. How many feet is that? (b) The cafeteria needs 23 quarts of milk each day. How many gallons is that? (c) The laundry detergent box weighed 128 ounces. How many pounds is that?

Home Involvement Activity

Directions: Use a map to find out how many miles you live from Winnipeg, Canada. Then change the measurement to yards, feet, and inches. Measure how tall you are in inches. Then change to feet and yards.

Teacher's Name _____ Class _____ Room _____ Date _____

LESSON 7.1

Lesson Plan

1-day lesson (See *Pacing and Assignment Guide*, TE page 310A)

For use with pages 313–317

GOAL Multiply fractions and whole numbers.

State/Local Objectives _____

_____

✓ **Check the items you wish to use for this lesson.**

STARTING OPTIONS

_____ Warm-Up: Transparencies

TEACHING OPTIONS

_____ Notetaking Guide

_____ Examples: 1–4, SE pages 313–315

_____ Extra Examples: TE pages 314–315

_____ Your Turn Now Exercises: 1–8, SE pages 314–315

_____ Concept Check: TE page 315

_____ Getting Ready to Practice Exercises: 1–10, SE page 315

APPLY/HOMEWORK

Homework Assignment

_____ Basic: Day 1: EP p. 712 Exs. 43–47; pp. 316–317 Exs. 11–30, 35–39, 42, 48–59

_____ Average: Day 1: pp. 316–317 Exs. 15–26, 31–44, 48–53, 57–59

_____ Advanced: Day 1: pp. 316–317 Exs. 17–26, 31–47*, 50–55, 59

Reteaching the Lesson

_____ Practice: CRB pages 7–9 (Level A, Level B, Level C); Practice Workbook

_____ Study Guide: CRB pages 10–11; Spanish Study Guide

Extending the Lesson

_____ Challenge: SE page 317; CRB page 12

ASSESSMENT OPTIONS

_____ Daily Quiz (7.1): TE page 317 or Transparencies

_____ Test Taking Practice: SE page 317

Notes _____

_____

_____

_____

_____

Lesson Plan for Block Scheduling

LESSON 7.1

Half-block lesson (See *Pacing and Assignment Guide*, TE page 310A)

For use with pages 313–317

GOAL Multiply fractions and whole numbers.

State/Local Objectives _____

_____

✓ Check the items you wish to use for this lesson.

Chapter Pacing Guide	
Day	**Lesson**
1	**7.1;** 7.2 (begin)
2	7.2 (end); 7.3
3	7.4; 7.5
4	7.6; 7.7
5	Ch. 7 Review and Projects

STARTING OPTIONS

____ Warm-Up: Transparencies

TEACHING OPTIONS

____ Notetaking Guide

____ Examples: 1–4, SE pages 313–315

____ Extra Examples: TE pages 314–315

____ Your Turn Now Exercises: 1–8, SE pages 314–315

____ Concept Check: TE page 315

____ Getting Ready to Practice Exercises: 1–10, SE page 315

APPLY/HOMEWORK

Homework Assignment

____ Block Schedule: pp. 316–317 Exs. 15–26, 31–44, 48–53, 57–59 (with 7.2)

Reteaching the Lesson

____ Practice: CRB pages 7–9 (Level A, Level B, Level C); Practice Workbook

____ Study Guide: CRB pages 10–11; Spanish Study Guide

Extending the Lesson

____ Challenge: SE page 317; CRB page 12

ASSESSMENT OPTIONS

____ Daily Quiz (7.1): TE page 317 or Transparencies

____ Test Taking Practice: SE page 317

Notes

_____

_____

_____

_____

Name _____ Date _____

Practice A

For use with pages 313–317

1. What multiplication problem does the model represent?

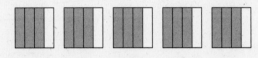

Find the product. Simplify if possible.

2. $\frac{3}{7} \times 2$

3. $5 \times \frac{1}{8}$

4. $\frac{3}{5} \times 5$

5. $8 \times \frac{1}{4}$

6. $\frac{8}{5} \times 6$

7. $24 \times \frac{2}{3}$

8. $\frac{4}{7} \times 12$

9. $5 \times \frac{1}{2}$

10. $\frac{8}{9} \times 10$

Identify the closest whole number that is compatible with the denominator of the fraction. Then estimate the answer.

11. $\frac{1}{6} \times 11$

12. $\frac{2}{3} \times 5$

13. $8 \times \frac{4}{5}$

14. $18 \times \frac{5}{8}$

15. $13 \times \frac{1}{4}$

16. $\frac{7}{10} \times 21$

Find the amount.

17. Number of minutes in $\frac{3}{4}$ of an hour

18. Number of inches in $\frac{7}{6}$ feet

19. Cost of $\frac{2}{3}$ pound of turkey at $6 per pound

20. You are bringing 30 cupcakes for your classmates on your birthday. You want $\frac{5}{6}$ of the cupcakes to be chocolate. How many chocolate cupcakes will you bring?

21. A man orders 1 dozen bagels. He wants $\frac{1}{4}$ of the bagels to be cinnamon raisin. How many of the bagels will be cinnamon raisin?

Name _____ Date _____

Practice B

For use with pages 313–317

1. What multiplication problem does the model represent?

Find the product. Simplify if possible.

2. $\frac{2}{3} \times 5$

3. $10 \times \frac{1}{2}$

4. $\frac{3}{5} \times 4$

5. $6 \times \frac{2}{9}$

6. $\frac{8}{13} \times 4$

7. $7 \times \frac{3}{4}$

8. $\frac{7}{8} \times 15$

9. $22 \times \frac{3}{11}$

10. $\frac{4}{7} \times 13$

Identify the closest whole number that is compatible with the denominator of the fraction. Then estimate the answer.

11. $\frac{2}{3} \times 7$

12. $\frac{4}{9} \times 17$

13. $10 \times \frac{5}{6}$

14. $25 \times \frac{1}{6}$

15. $31 \times \frac{4}{5}$

16. $\frac{7}{9} \times 15$

17. You received $100 for your birthday. Your mother says that you need to save $\frac{2}{5}$ of the money. How much money do you need to save?

18. A softball team wins $\frac{5}{8}$ of their 32 games. How many games did they win? How many did they lose?

19. A group of 42 people went to the theater. In the group, $\frac{4}{7}$ of the people purchased a child's ticket and $\frac{1}{6}$ of the people purchased a senior citizen's ticket. How many of the people in the group were children and how many were senior citizens?

20. In a fish bowl there are 54 fish, $\frac{5}{9}$ of which are goldfish. How many goldfish are in the bowl?

Name _____ Date _____

Practice C
For use with pages 313–317

Find the product. Simplify if possible.

1. $\frac{2}{5} \times 8$

2. $9 \times \frac{1}{7}$

3. $\frac{3}{4} \times 5$

4. $7 \times \frac{8}{9}$

5. $\frac{6}{11} \times 3$

6. $12 \times \frac{5}{8}$

7. $\frac{5}{12} \times 17$

8. $21 \times \frac{1}{6}$

9. $\frac{12}{5} \times 11$

Identify the closest whole number that is compatible with the denominator of the fraction. Then estimate the answer.

10. $\frac{2}{5} \times 9$

11. $\frac{3}{4} \times 13$

12. $20 \times \frac{5}{6}$

13. $19 \times \frac{3}{7}$

14. $35 \times \frac{11}{12}$

15. $\frac{7}{9} \times 20$

Use the commutative and associative properties to find the product.

16. $16 \times \left(\frac{3}{8} \times 13 \right)$

17. $21 \times 5 \times \frac{4}{7}$

18. $\frac{6}{13} \times 7 \times 39$

19. Predict whether the product of 45 and each of the following fractions is *less than 45* or *greater than 45*: $\frac{1}{3}, \frac{2}{3}, \frac{4}{5}, \frac{7}{5}, \frac{5}{9}, \frac{10}{9}, \frac{11}{15}$. Then find the product to check your answer.

In Exercises 20–23, use the table that shows the fraction of each type of tree in a park that has 200 trees.

20. How many maple trees are in the park?

21. How many dogwood trees are in the park?

22. How many elm and maple trees are in the park?

23. What is the difference in the number of dogwood and pine trees in the park?

Tree Type	Fraction
Maple	$\frac{1}{20}$
Pine	$\frac{1}{5}$
Dogwood	$\frac{1}{2}$
Elm	$\frac{1}{4}$

24. You and a friend exchanged baseball cards. You gave your friend $\frac{3}{8}$ of a collection of 24 cards. Your friend gave you $\frac{4}{9}$ of a collection of 36 cards. How many cards do you each have now?

7.1 Study Guide

For use with pages 313–317

GOAL Multiply fractions and whole numbers.

> **VOCABULARY**
>
> **Multiplying Fractions by Whole Numbers**
>
> **Words** To multiply a fraction by a whole number, multiply the numerator of the fraction by the whole number and write the product over the original denominator. Simplify if possible.
>
> **Numbers** $3 \times \frac{2}{5} = \frac{6}{5}$ **Algebra** $x \cdot \frac{y}{z} = \frac{x \cdot y}{z}$

EXAMPLE 1 Multiply Fractions by Whole Numbers

$$4 \times \frac{5}{8} = \frac{4 \times 5}{8}$$ Multiply the numerator by the whole number.

$$= \frac{20}{8}$$

$$= \frac{5}{2}, \text{ or } 2\frac{1}{2}$$ Simplify.

Exercises for Example 1

Find the product. Simplify if possible.

1. $5 \times \frac{2}{3}$ **2.** $2 \times \frac{3}{4}$ **3.** $4 \times \frac{3}{5}$

4. $2 \times \frac{7}{8}$ **5.** $3 \times \frac{5}{6}$ **6.** $9 \times \frac{2}{3}$

EXAMPLE 2 Multiply Whole Numbers by Fractions

a. $\frac{7}{10} \times 2 = \frac{14}{10}$ **b.** $\frac{3}{8} \times 4 = \frac{12}{8}$

$= \frac{7}{5}, \text{ or } 1\frac{2}{5}$ $= \frac{3}{2}, \text{ or } 1\frac{1}{2}$

Exercises for Example 2

Find the product. Simplify if possible.

7. $\frac{2}{3} \times 4$ **8.** $\frac{3}{2} \times 3$ **9.** $\frac{1}{6} \times 7$

10. $\frac{1}{6} \times 9$ **11.** $\frac{5}{8} \times 4$ **12.** $\frac{3}{4} \times 3$

Name _____ Date _____

Study Guide

For use with pages 313–317

EXAMPLE 3 Using Mental Math or a Model

You are making 12 kites. You need $\frac{3}{4}$ yard of fabric for each kite.
How many yards of fabric do you need?

Solution

The number of yards of fabric that you need is $\frac{3}{4} \times 12$, or $\frac{3}{4}$ *of* 12.

You can use a model or mental math to find this product.

Method 1: Use a model. Draw 12 circles.
Divide them into four equal parts. Circle
three of the four parts.

 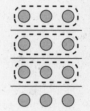

Method 2: Use mental math. Think: $\frac{1}{4}$ of 12
is 3, because $12 \div 4 = 3$. So, $\frac{3}{4}$ of 12 is 9
because $3 \times 3 = 9$.

Answer: You need 9 yards of fabric.

Exercises for Example 3

Use a model to find the product.

13. $\frac{1}{4} \times 20$ **14.** $\frac{1}{3} \times 9$ **15.** $\frac{2}{5} \times 20$

Use mental math to find the product.

16. $\frac{2}{5} \times 10$ **17.** $\frac{5}{6} \times 18$ **18.** $\frac{3}{4} \times 8$

EXAMPLE 4 Estimating a Product

Estimate $\frac{2}{3} \times 11$.

$\frac{2}{3} \times 11 \approx \frac{2}{3} \times 12$ Replace 11 with a number compatible with 3.

≈ 8 **Think:** $\frac{1}{3}$ of 12 is 4, so $\frac{2}{3}$ of 12 is 8.

Exercises for Example 4

Use compatible numbers to estimate the product.

19. $\frac{1}{3} \times 10$ **20.** $\frac{1}{4} \times 17$ **21.** $\frac{1}{5} \times 11$

22. $\frac{2}{3} \times 14$ **23.** $\frac{4}{5} \times 6$ **24.** $\frac{3}{4} \times 13$

Name _____ Date _____

Challenge Practice

For use with pages 313–317

Find the water pressure at the depth of each shipwreck. Use the formula $P = \frac{5}{11}D + 15$, where P is the pressure of sea water in psi (pounds per square inch) and D is the depth below the surface in feet.

1. The Lusitania, a British steamship, sank in 18 minutes just south of Ireland to a depth of 295 feet.

2. The Titanic, the luxurious passenger ship, sank on its maiden voyage to a depth of 12,460 feet.

3. The Empress of Ireland, a Canadian steamship, collided with another ship due to fog and sank to a depth of 150 feet.

4. The Britannic, a British hospital ship, sank at the end of World War I to a depth of 395 feet.

5. The Andrea Doria, the Italian luxury and "unsinkable" ship, sank in New York harbor to a depth of 225 feet.

LESSON
7.2

Lesson Plan

2-day lesson (See *Pacing and Assignment Guide*, TE page 310A)

For use with pages 318–325

GOAL **Multiply fractions.**

State/Local Objectives _____

_____

✓ Check the items you wish to use for this lesson.

STARTING OPTIONS

_____ Homework Check (7.1): TE page 316; Answer Transparencies

_____ Homework Quiz (7.1): TE page 317; Transparencies

_____ Warm-Up: Transparencies

TEACHING OPTIONS

_____ Notetaking Guide

_____ Hands-on Activity: SE pages 318–319

_____ Activity Support Master: CRB page 15

_____ Examples: Day 1: 1–3, SE pages 320–321; Day 2: 4–5, SE page 322

_____ Extra Examples: TE pages 321–322

_____ Your Turn Now Exercises: Day 1: 1–8, SE pages 320–321; Day 2: 9–15, SE page 322

_____ Concept Check: TE page 322

_____ Getting Ready to Practice Exercises: Day 1: Exs. 1–8, SE page 323; Day 2: Ex. 9, SE page 323

APPLY/HOMEWORK

Homework Assignment

_____ Basic: Day 1: EP p. 712 Exs. 16–19; pp. 323–325 Exs. 10–14, 19–22, 37–39, 52–57
Day 2: pp. 323–325 Exs. 23–31, 36, 43–47, 60–62

_____ Average: Day 1: pp. 323–325 Exs. 10–12, 17–22, 40–45, 54–57
Day 2: pp. 323–325 Exs. 27–36, 46–50, 61–63

_____ Advanced: Day 1: pp. 323–325 Exs. 10, 15–22, 40–46, 52–55
Day 2: pp. 323–325 Exs. 29–36, 47–51*, 58–63

Reteaching the Lesson

_____ Practice: CRB pages 16–18 (Level A, Level B, Level C); Practice Workbook

_____ Study Guide: CRB pages 19–20; Spanish Study Guide

Extending the Lesson

_____ Challenge: SE page 325; CRB page 21

ASSESSMENT OPTIONS

_____ Daily Quiz (7.2): TE page 325 or Transparencies

_____ Test Taking Practice: SE page 325

Notes _____

Lesson 7.2

LESSON 7.2 Lesson Plan for Block Scheduling

1-block lesson (See *Pacing and Assignment Guide*, TE page 310A)

For use with pages 318–325

GOAL Multiply fractions.

State/Local Objectives _____

_____

✓ **Check the items you wish to use for this lesson.**

Chapter Pacing Guide	
Day	**Lesson**
1	7.1; **7.2 (begin)**
2	**7.2 (end)**; 7.3
3	7.4; 7.5
4	7.6; 7.7
5	Ch. 7 Review and Projects

STARTING OPTIONS

____ Homework Check (7.1): TE page 316; Answer Transparencies

____ Homework Quiz (7.1): TE page 317; Transparencies

____ Warm-Up: Transparencies

TEACHING OPTIONS

____ Notetaking Guide

____ Hands-on Activity: SE pages 318–319

____ Activity Support Master: CRB page 15

____ Examples: Day 1: 1–3, SE pages 320–321; Day 2: 4–5, SE page 322

____ Extra Examples: TE pages 321–322

____ Your Turn Now Exercises: Day 1: 1–8, SE pages 320–321; Day 2: 9–15, SE page 322

____ Concept Check: TE page 322

____ Getting Ready to Practice Exercises: Day 1: Exs. 1–8, SE page 323; Day 2: Ex. 9, SE page 323

APPLY/HOMEWORK

Homework Assignment

____ Block Schedule: Day 1: pp. 323–325 Exs. 10–12, 17–22, 40–45, 54–57 (with 7.1)
Day 2: pp. 323–325 Exs. 27–36, 46–50, 61–63 (with 7.3)

Reteaching the Lesson

____ Practice: CRB pages 16–18 (Level A, Level B, Level C); Practice Workbook

____ Study Guide: CRB pages 19–20; Spanish Study Guide

Extending the Lesson

____ Challenge: SE page 325; CRB page 21

ASSESSMENT OPTIONS

____ Daily Quiz (7.2): TE page 325 or Transparencies

____ Test Taking Practice: SE page 325

Notes _____

_____

_____

Name _____ Date _____

Activity Support Master

For use with page 318

Name _____ Date _____

Practice A

For use with pages 318–325

1. Draw a model to find the product $\frac{1}{3} \times \frac{4}{7}$.

Find the product. Write the answer in simplest form.

2. $\frac{2}{5} \times \frac{1}{6}$

3. $\frac{1}{8} \times \frac{3}{7}$

4. $\frac{2}{5} \times \frac{5}{9}$

5. $\frac{7}{10} \times \frac{1}{2}$

6. $\frac{2}{3} \times \frac{4}{7}$

7. $\frac{1}{6} \times \frac{2}{3}$

8. $\frac{5}{11} \times \frac{1}{4}$

9. $\frac{3}{8} \times \frac{3}{4}$

10. $\frac{1}{2} \times \frac{7}{9}$

Evaluate the expression when $x = \frac{1}{6}$.

11. $\frac{5}{8}x$

12. $\frac{3}{4}x$

13. $\frac{9}{11}x$

14. Find the product of $\frac{1}{9}$ and $\frac{7}{12}$.

15. Find $\frac{1}{7}$ of $\frac{2}{9}$.

16. Evaluate $\frac{16}{21}m$ when $m = \frac{2}{5}$.

17. Find $\frac{6}{19}$ of $\frac{4}{9}$.

18. You are biking in a race that is $\frac{3}{4}$ of a mile long and you are $\frac{1}{3}$ of the way finished. How much of the race have you biked?

19. The recipe for a batch of brownies calls for $\frac{1}{2}$ cup of oil. You only want to make $\frac{1}{4}$ of a batch. How much oil do you need?

20. A pattern for curtains calls for $\frac{3}{8}$ of a yard of material. You want to shorten the curtains to $\frac{2}{5}$ of the height on the pattern. How much fabric do you need?

Lesson 7.2

Name _____ Date _____

Practice B

For use with pages 318–325

1. What multiplication problem does the model represent?

Find the product. Write the answer in simplest form.

2. $\dfrac{4}{6} \times \dfrac{2}{5}$

3. $\dfrac{1}{4} \times \dfrac{3}{7}$

4. $\dfrac{9}{10} \times \dfrac{1}{3}$

5. $\dfrac{7}{8} \times \dfrac{1}{2}$

6. $\dfrac{2}{3} \times \dfrac{6}{11}$

7. $\dfrac{4}{5} \times \dfrac{3}{4}$

8. $\dfrac{5}{6} \times \dfrac{11}{12}$

9. $\dfrac{3}{8} \times \dfrac{5}{6} \times \dfrac{1}{3}$

10. $\dfrac{5}{7} \times \dfrac{8}{9} \times \dfrac{6}{11}$

Evaluate the expression when $x = \dfrac{2}{3}$.

11. $\dfrac{3}{4}x$

12. $\dfrac{7}{9}x$

13. $\dfrac{11}{16}x$

Complete the statement using <, >, or =.

14. $\dfrac{2}{3} \times \dfrac{7}{9}$ ___?___ 1

15. $\dfrac{4}{5} \times \dfrac{9}{7}$ ___?___ $\dfrac{4}{5}$

16. $\dfrac{2}{5} \times \dfrac{1}{9}$ ___?___ $\dfrac{2}{5}$

17. $\dfrac{6}{11} \times \dfrac{10}{10}$ ___?___ $\dfrac{6}{11}$

18. $\dfrac{1}{8} \times \dfrac{5}{8}$ ___?___ $\dfrac{1}{8}$

19. $\dfrac{1}{8} \times \dfrac{5}{8}$ ___?___ $\dfrac{5}{8}$

In Exercises 20–22, use the following information. A teacher allows $\dfrac{5}{6}$ of an hour to be spent on homework in class.

20. She wants to spend $\dfrac{1}{3}$ of that time on math. How much time will be spent doing math homework?

21. She wants to spend $\dfrac{1}{2}$ of the time on English. How much time will be spent doing English homework?

22. The remaining time is to be spent on science. How much time will be spent on science homework?

Name _____ Date _____

Practice C

For use with pages 318–325

Find the product. Write the answer in simplest form.

1. $\dfrac{2}{5} \times \dfrac{5}{8}$

2. $\dfrac{3}{4} \times \dfrac{11}{12}$

3. $\dfrac{8}{9} \times \dfrac{5}{7}$

4. $\dfrac{4}{5} \times \dfrac{2}{9}$

5. $\dfrac{3}{10} \times \dfrac{8}{11}$

6. $\dfrac{15}{12} \times \dfrac{7}{18}$

7. $\dfrac{5}{6} \times \dfrac{3}{4} \times \dfrac{2}{5}$

8. $\dfrac{7}{8} \times \dfrac{5}{9} \times \dfrac{1}{3}$

9. $\dfrac{3}{14} \times \dfrac{8}{15} \times \dfrac{5}{6}$

Evaluate the expression when $x = \dfrac{5}{7}$.

10. $\dfrac{3}{8}x$

11. $\dfrac{4}{11}x$

12. $\dfrac{7}{12}x$

Complete the statement using <, >, or =.

13. $\dfrac{3}{4} \times \dfrac{8}{9} \underline{} 1$

14. $\dfrac{5}{9} \times \dfrac{3}{11} \underline{} \dfrac{5}{9}$

15. $\dfrac{6}{7} \times \dfrac{2}{2} \underline{} \dfrac{6}{7}$

16. $\dfrac{9}{16} \times \dfrac{23}{21} \underline{} \dfrac{9}{16}$

17. $\dfrac{11}{12} \times \dfrac{14}{15} \underline{} \dfrac{11}{12}$

18. $\dfrac{6}{7} \times \dfrac{2}{2} \underline{} \dfrac{1}{2}$

Evaluate the expression.

19. $\dfrac{1}{5} + \dfrac{2}{5} \times \dfrac{1}{2}$

20. $\dfrac{8}{9} - \dfrac{1}{9} \times \dfrac{1}{4}$

21. $\dfrac{1}{6} \times \left(\dfrac{4}{7}\right)^2$

Find the product.

22. $\dfrac{8}{35} \times \dfrac{7}{40} \times \dfrac{12}{38}$

23. $\dfrac{21}{78} \times \dfrac{29}{42} \times \dfrac{50}{87}$

24. $\dfrac{28}{45} \times \dfrac{32}{55} \times \dfrac{36}{64}$

25. Use number sense to order the expressions from *least* to *greatest* without finding the products. Explain how you decided.

$\dfrac{5}{6} \times \dfrac{8}{9} \qquad \dfrac{5}{6} \times \dfrac{3}{16} \qquad \dfrac{5}{6} \times \dfrac{1}{2} \qquad \dfrac{21}{20} \times \dfrac{5}{6} \qquad \dfrac{5}{6} \times \dfrac{1}{30}$

26. In a survey of 600 families, $\dfrac{5}{8}$ of the families said that they took a summer vacation. Of those families, $\dfrac{2}{5}$ said they went on a camping trip. How many families went camping on their summer vacation?

Name _____ Date _____

Study Guide
For use with pages 318–325

GOAL **Multiply fractions.**

> **Multiplying Fractions**
>
> $$\text{product of fractions} = \frac{\text{product of numerators}}{\text{product of denominators}}$$

EXAMPLE 1 **Using a Model to Multiply Fractions**

Draw a model to find $\frac{1}{2} \times \frac{3}{4}$.

(1) Draw a 2 by 4 rectangle to model halves and fourths. Each small square is $\frac{1}{8}$ of the whole.

(2) Shade $\frac{3}{4}$ of the rectangle.

(3) Select $\frac{1}{2}$ of the shaded rectangle.

Answer: Three of the 8 squares are selected, so $\frac{1}{2} \times \frac{3}{4} = \frac{3}{8}$.

Exercises for Example 1

Draw a model to find the product.

1. $\frac{1}{4} \times \frac{1}{3}$ **2.** $\frac{1}{3} \times \frac{2}{5}$ **3.** $\frac{1}{2} \times \frac{5}{6}$

EXAMPLE 2 **Multiplying Two Fractions**

$\frac{1}{2} \times \frac{3}{5} = \frac{1 \times 3}{2 \times 5}$ Use the rule for multiplying fractions.

$= \frac{3}{10}$ Multiply. The product is in simplest form.

Exercises for Example 2

Find the product.

4. $\frac{1}{8} \times \frac{3}{4}$ **5.** $\frac{1}{2} \times \frac{1}{2}$ **6.** $\frac{4}{5} \times \frac{2}{3}$

7. $\frac{1}{4} \times \frac{5}{7}$ **8.** $\frac{4}{9} \times \frac{1}{3}$ **9.** $\frac{5}{6} \times \frac{1}{2}$

Lesson 7.2

Name _____ Date _____

Study Guide

For use with pages 318–325

EXAMPLE 3 **Evaluating an Algebraic Expression**

Evaluate the expression $\frac{4}{5}y$ when $y = \frac{1}{3}$.

$\frac{4}{5}y = \frac{4}{5} \times \frac{1}{3}$ Substitute $\frac{1}{3}$ for y.

$= \frac{4 \times 1}{5 \times 3}$ Use the rule for multiplying fractions.

$= \frac{4}{15}$ Multiply. The product is in simplest form.

Exercises for Example 3

Evaluate the expression when $x = \frac{1}{4}$.

10. $\frac{1}{5}x$ **11.** $\frac{5}{9}x$ **12.** $\frac{3}{7}x$

EXAMPLE 4 **Simplifying Before Multiplying**

$\frac{2}{3} \times \frac{9}{20} = \frac{2 \times 9}{3 \times 20}$ Use the rule for multiplying fractions.

$= \frac{2 \times \overset{1}{\overset{}{9}}\overset{3}{}}{\underset{1}{3} \times \underset{10}{20}}$ 3 is a factor of 3 and 9. Divide 9 and 3 by 3. Also, 2 is a factor of 2 and 20. Divide 2 and 20 by 2.

$= \frac{1 \times 3}{1 \times 10}$ Rewrite.

$= \frac{3}{10}$ Multiply.

EXAMPLE 5 **Multiplying Three Fractions**

$\frac{2}{7} \times \frac{1}{6} \times \frac{3}{10} = \frac{2 \times 1 \times 3}{7 \times 6 \times 10}$ Use the rule for multiplying fractions.

$= \frac{\overset{1}{2} \times 1 \times \overset{1}{3}}{7 \times \underset{2}{6} \times \underset{5}{10}}$ 2 is a factor of 2 and 10. Divide 2 and 10 by 2. 3 is a factor of 3 and 6. Divide 3 and 6 by 3.

$= \frac{1 \times 1 \times 1}{7 \times 2 \times 5}$ Rewrite.

$= \frac{1}{70}$ Multiply.

Exercises for Examples 4 and 5

Multiply. Write the answer in simplest form.

13. $\frac{2}{7} \times \frac{3}{4}$ **14.** $\frac{3}{5} \times \frac{5}{3}$ **15.** $\frac{3}{5} \times \frac{4}{9} \times \frac{5}{8}$

Lesson 7.2

Name _____ Date _____

Challenge Practice

For use with pages 318–325

Write the multiplication problem shown in the model.

1.

2.

3.

4.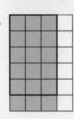

Find the product.

5. $\dfrac{5}{6} \times \dfrac{48}{77} \times \dfrac{7}{24} \times \dfrac{33}{25}$

6. $\dfrac{7}{12} \times \dfrac{2}{21} \times \dfrac{36}{49} \times \dfrac{7}{18}$

7. $\dfrac{18}{19} \times \dfrac{38}{49} \times \dfrac{21}{40} \times \dfrac{25}{54}$

8. $\dfrac{9}{25} \times \dfrac{5}{6} \times \dfrac{18}{49} \times \dfrac{35}{81}$

9. Show that the sum and the product of the fractions $\dfrac{13}{4}$ and $\dfrac{13}{9}$ are the same. Do you think that this is true for any two fractions? Explain your answer using examples.

LESSON 7.3

Lesson Plan

1-day lesson (See *Pacing and Assignment Guide*, TE page 310A)

For use with pages 326–330

GOAL **Multiply mixed numbers.**

State/Local Objectives _____

_____

✓ **Check the items you wish to use for this lesson.**

STARTING OPTIONS

_____ Homework Check (7.2): TE page 323; Answer Transparencies

_____ Homework Quiz (7.2): TE page 325; Transparencies

_____ Warm-Up: Transparencies

TEACHING OPTIONS

_____ Notetaking Guide

_____ Examples: 1–3, SE pages 326–327

_____ Extra Examples: TE page 327

_____ Your Turn Now Exercises: 1–4, SE page 327

_____ Concept Check: TE page 327

_____ Getting Ready to Practice Exercises: 1–10, SE page 328

APPLY/HOMEWORK

Homework Assignment

_____ Basic: Day 1: EP p. 712 Exs. 38–42; pp. 328–330 Exs. 11–22, 27–33, 36–41, 48–53

_____ Average: Day 1: pp. 328–330 Exs. 19–26, 29–37, 40–46, 49–54

_____ Advanced: Day 1: pp. 328–330 Exs. 21–28, 31–35, 38–50*, 53, 54

Reteaching the Lesson

_____ Practice: CRB pages 24–26 (Level A, Level B, Level C); Practice Workbook

_____ Study Guide: CRB pages 27–28; Spanish Study Guide

Extending the Lesson

_____ Challenge: SE page 329; CRB page 29

ASSESSMENT OPTIONS

_____ Daily Quiz (7.3): TE page 330 or Transparencies

_____ Test Taking Practice: SE page 330

_____ Quiz (7.1–7.3): SE page 332; Assessment Book page 79

Notes _____

_____

_____

Lesson 7.3

LESSON

7.3

Lesson Plan for Block Scheduling

Half-block lesson (See *Pacing and Assignment Guide*, TE page 310A)

For use with pages 326–330

GOAL **Multiply mixed numbers.**

State/Local Objectives _____

_____

✓ Check the items you wish to use for this lesson.

Chapter Pacing Guide	
Day	**Lesson**
1	7.1; 7.2 (begin)
2	7.2 (end); **7.3**
3	7.4; 7.5
4	7.6; 7.7
5	Ch. 7 Review and Projects

STARTING OPTIONS

____ Homework Check (7.2): TE page 323; Answer Transparencies

____ Homework Quiz (7.2): TE page 325; Transparencies

____ Warm-Up: Transparencies

TEACHING OPTIONS

____ Notetaking Guide

____ Examples: 1–3, SE pages 326–327

____ Extra Examples: TE page 327

____ Your Turn Now Exercises: 1–4, SE page 327

____ Concept Check: TE page 327

____ Getting Ready to Practice Exercises: 1–10, SE page 328

APPLY/HOMEWORK

Homework Assignment

____ Block Schedule: pp. 328–330 Exs. 19–26, 29–37, 40–46, 49–54 (with 7.2)

Reteaching the Lesson

____ Practice: CRB pages 24–26 (Level A, Level B, Level C); Practice Workbook

____ Study Guide: CRB pages 27–28; Spanish Study Guide

Extending the Lesson

____ Challenge: SE page 329; CRB page 29

ASSESSMENT OPTIONS

____ Daily Quiz (7.3): TE page 330 or Transparencies

____ Test Taking Practice: SE page 330

____ Quiz (7.1–7.3): SE page 332; Assessment Book page 79

Notes

_____

_____

_____

Lesson 7.3

Find the product. Write the answer in simplest form.

1. $1\frac{3}{8} \times \frac{1}{3}$

2. $2\frac{1}{5} \times \frac{1}{6}$

3. $3 \times 4\frac{2}{3}$

4. $1\frac{1}{2} \times 2\frac{4}{5}$

5. $8\frac{2}{7} \times 3\frac{1}{4}$

6. $\frac{11}{12} \times 3\frac{5}{8}$

7. $7\frac{1}{6} \times 6\frac{3}{5}$

8. $12 \times \frac{6}{7}$

9. $1\frac{2}{3} \times 1\frac{1}{8}$

10. $5\frac{3}{7} \times 2$

11. $8 \times \frac{7}{10}$

12. $6 \times 2\frac{7}{8}$

Tell whether you can simplify before multiplying. If so, tell how.

13. $\frac{6}{7} \times \frac{1}{3}$

14. $\frac{8}{3} \times \frac{8}{5}$

15. $\frac{10}{15} \times \frac{3}{12}$

Use rounding to estimate the product.

16. $4\frac{2}{3} \times 3\frac{1}{8}$

17. $7 \times 6\frac{10}{11}$

18. $2\frac{1}{7} \times 3\frac{1}{4}$

Find the area of the rectangle.

19.
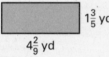
$1\frac{3}{5}$ yd

$4\frac{2}{9}$ yd

20.

$2\frac{1}{4}$ m

$3\frac{3}{8}$ m

21. Mike can run 1 mile in $4\frac{1}{2}$ minutes. How long will it take him to run $6\frac{5}{9}$ miles?

22. Cheryl earns $5\frac{3}{4}$ dollars an hour for babysitting. How much money will she earn if she babysits for $3\frac{3}{5}$ hours?

23. Anita is making a tablecloth. The table is $7\frac{5}{12}$ feet long by $3\frac{3}{4}$ feet wide. How much fabric is needed to make the tablecloth?

Lesson 7.3

Name _____ Date _____

Practice B
For use with pages 326–330

Find the product. Write the answer in simplest form.

1. $2\frac{3}{8} \times \frac{2}{3}$

2. $1\frac{4}{5} \times \frac{1}{2}$

3. $3 \times 2\frac{4}{9}$

4. $4 \times 6\frac{1}{5}$

5. $5\frac{7}{9} \times 3\frac{2}{11}$

6. $1\frac{1}{4} \times 1\frac{2}{7}$

7. $6\frac{2}{9} \times 4\frac{1}{3}$

8. $24 \times \frac{1}{6}$

9. $12\frac{3}{10} \times \frac{5}{8}$

10. $\frac{3}{7} \times 35$

11. $9\frac{2}{11} \times 3\frac{6}{17}$

12. $7\frac{4}{15} \times 3\frac{5}{21}$

Use rounding to estimate the product.

13. $5 \times 3\frac{7}{8}$

14. $1\frac{2}{5} \times 3\frac{9}{10}$

15. $4\frac{3}{13} \times 4\frac{1}{12}$

Find the area of the rectangle.

16.

$2\frac{5}{7}$ cm

$6\frac{4}{11}$ cm

17.

$\frac{9}{13}$ ft

$3\frac{1}{3}$ ft

In Exercises 18–20, use the table that shows the trails in Mt. Diablo State Park in Walnut Creek, California.

Trail	Length (miles)
Donner Creek	$\frac{9}{10}$
Castle Rock	$1\frac{1}{2}$
Summit Loop	$\frac{7}{10}$
Pine Pond	$1\frac{3}{5}$

18. A visitor hiked Castle Rock trail $2\frac{1}{3}$ times. How many miles did he hike?

19. A walker decided to walk Summit Loop twice and Donner Creek three times. How many miles did she walk?

20. What is the combined distance of the four trails?

A jogger decided to run all four trails $3\frac{1}{2}$ times. How many miles did the jogger run?

Name _____ Date _____

Practice C

For use with pages 326–330

Find the product. Write the answer in simplest form.

1. $3\frac{3}{7} \times 2\frac{1}{3}$ **2.** $2\frac{3}{5} \times \frac{6}{7}$

3. $3 \times 1\frac{5}{8}$ **4.** $2 \times 3\frac{4}{5}$

5. $7\frac{1}{6} \times 2\frac{4}{13}$ **6.** $1\frac{4}{11} \times 3\frac{4}{7}$

7. $5\frac{5}{9} \times 3\frac{2}{5}$ **8.** $13 \times 2\frac{1}{5}$

9. $14\frac{7}{12} \times 3\frac{3}{4}$ **10.** $\frac{8}{9} \times 25$

11. $10\frac{7}{8} \times 12\frac{20}{21}$ **12.** $17\frac{3}{16} \times 4\frac{15}{22}$

Use rounding to estimate the product.

13. $11 \times 2\frac{1}{7}$ **14.** $6\frac{3}{4} \times 5\frac{12}{13}$ **15.** $8\frac{4}{15} \times 2\frac{1}{13}$

Find the area of the rectangle.

16.

$2\frac{2}{9}$ m

$4\frac{3}{5}$ m

17.

$4\frac{4}{11}$ in.

$5\frac{6}{7}$ in.

18. Find the product of $3\frac{14}{15} \times \frac{9}{26} \times 13 \times 2\frac{6}{27}$.

19. An author has a goal of writing 300 pages in 24 days. He can write $12\frac{2}{9}$ pages per day. Will the author reach his goal?

20. A fabric costs $13\frac{3}{16}$ dollars per yard. You want to purchase $14\frac{1}{4}$ yards. How much will the fabric cost?

21. Susan is taking a 700-mile trip. Her car takes $12\frac{2}{7}$ gallons of gasoline and can go 29 miles per gallon. How many miles can she go on a full tank? How many times will she have to fill her tank for the trip?

Lesson 7.3

LESSON 7.3

Study Guide

For use with pages 326–330

GOAL Multiply mixed numbers.

VOCABULARY

When finding a product involving a mixed number, it is helpful to first write all the numbers in fraction form.

EXAMPLE 1 **Multiplying with Mixed Numbers**

a. $\dfrac{3}{4} \times 1\dfrac{1}{4} = \dfrac{3}{4} \times \dfrac{5}{4}$ Write $1\dfrac{1}{4}$ as an improper fraction.

$= \dfrac{3 \times 5}{4 \times 4}$ Use the rule for multiplying fractions.

$= \dfrac{15}{16}$ Multiply. The answer is in simplest form.

b. $2\dfrac{2}{3} \times 4 = \dfrac{8}{3} \times \dfrac{4}{1}$ Write $2\dfrac{2}{3}$ and 4 as improper fractions.

$= \dfrac{8 \times 4}{3 \times 1}$ Use the rule for multiplying fractions.

$= \dfrac{32}{3}$, or $10\dfrac{2}{3}$ Multiply. The answer is in simplest form.

Exercises for Example 1

Multiply. Write the answer in simplest form.

1. $\dfrac{3}{5} \times 1\dfrac{1}{2}$ **2.** $3\dfrac{1}{3} \times \dfrac{2}{7}$ **3.** $2\dfrac{1}{3} \times \dfrac{4}{5}$

4. $\dfrac{3}{10} \times 1\dfrac{1}{4}$ **5.** $1\dfrac{3}{4} \times 3$ **6.** $3 \times 4\dfrac{1}{2}$

EXAMPLE 2 **Simplifying Before Multiplying**

$4\dfrac{1}{5} \times 3\dfrac{1}{3} = \dfrac{21}{5} \times \dfrac{10}{3}$ Write $4\dfrac{1}{5}$ and $3\dfrac{1}{3}$ as improper fractions.

$= \dfrac{\overset{7}{\cancel{21}} \times \overset{2}{\cancel{10}}}{\underset{1}{\cancel{5}} \times \underset{1}{\cancel{3}}}$ Use the rule for multiplying fractions. Divide out common factors.

$= \dfrac{7 \times 2}{1 \times 1}$ Rewrite.

$= \dfrac{14}{1}$ Multiply.

$= 14$ Write the answer in simplest form.

Lesson 7.3

Name _____ Date _____

Study Guide

For use with pages 326–330

Exercises for Example 2

Multiply. Write the answer in simplest form.

7. $3\frac{1}{3} \times 4\frac{1}{2}$

8. $1\frac{1}{5} \times 3\frac{1}{3}$

9. $2\frac{1}{4} \times 1\frac{1}{3}$

10. $1\frac{1}{4} \times 1\frac{3}{5}$

11. $4\frac{1}{2} \times 3\frac{1}{9}$

12. $3\frac{1}{5} \times 4\frac{1}{6}$

EXAMPLE 3 **Multiplying to Solve Problems**

A rectangular flower garden measures $6\frac{2}{5}$ feet by $5\frac{5}{6}$ feet. What is the area of the garden?

Solution

$\quad$ Area = **Length** × **Width**

$\quad\quad = 6\frac{2}{5} \times 5\frac{5}{6}$ $\quad\quad\quad$ Substitute for length and width.

$\quad\quad = \frac{32}{5} \times \frac{35}{6}$ $\quad\quad\quad$ Write $6\frac{2}{5}$ and $5\frac{5}{6}$ as improper fractions.

$\quad\quad = \dfrac{\overset{16}{\cancel{32}} \times \overset{7}{\cancel{35}}}{\underset{1}{\cancel{5}} \times \underset{3}{\cancel{6}}}$ $\quad\quad\quad$ Use the rule for multiplying fractions. Divide out common factors.

$\quad\quad = \frac{16 \times 7}{1 \times 3}$ $\quad\quad\quad$ Rewrite.

$\quad\quad = \frac{112}{3}$, or $37\frac{1}{3}$ $\quad\quad\quad$ Multiply. The answer is in simplest form.

Answer: The area of the garden is $37\frac{1}{3}$ square feet.

Exercises for Example 3

Find the area of the rectangle.

13. 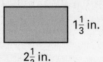 $1\frac{1}{3}$ in.
$2\frac{1}{2}$ in.

14. 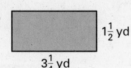 $1\frac{1}{2}$ yd
$3\frac{1}{4}$ yd

15. 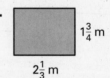 $1\frac{3}{4}$ m
$2\frac{1}{3}$ m

Lesson 7.3

Challenge Practice

For use with pages 326–330

In Exercises 1–8, use the timetable that gives the suggested roasting times in hours per pound for different meats at a cooking temperature of 325°F.

1. How long should you roast a whole ham that weighs $11\frac{2}{3}$ pounds?

2. At what time should you put the ham in the oven if you want to eat at 5:20 P.M.?

3. How long should you roast a chicken that weighs $3\frac{2}{3}$ pounds?

4. At what time should you put the chicken in the oven if you want to eat at 5:45 P.M.?

5. How long should you roast a pork roast that weighs $3\frac{4}{5}$ pounds?

Cooking Timetable	
Meat	**Time (hour per lb)**
Pork Roast	$\frac{7}{15}$
Ham	$\frac{1}{5}$
Beef Roast	$\frac{1}{3}$
Beef Ribs	$\frac{2}{5}$
Chicken	$1\frac{3}{4}$

6. At what time should you put the pork roast in the oven if you want to eat at 6:30 P.M.?

7. How long should you roast beef ribs that weigh $6\frac{1}{3}$ pounds?

8. How long should you roast a beef roast that weighs $8\frac{2}{5}$ pounds?

LESSON 7.4

Lesson Plan

1-day lesson (See *Pacing and Assignment Guide*, TE page 310A)

For use with pages 333–338

GOAL Use reciprocals to divide fractions.

State/Local Objectives _____

_____

✓ Check the items you wish to use for this lesson.

STARTING OPTIONS

_____ Homework Check (7.3): TE page 328; Answer Transparencies

_____ Homework Quiz (7.3): TE page 330; Transparencies

_____ Warm-Up: Transparencies

TEACHING OPTIONS

_____ Notetaking Guide

_____ Hands-on Activity: SE page 333

_____ Examples: 1–3, SE pages 334–335

_____ Extra Examples: TE page 335

_____ Your Turn Now Exercises: 1–8, SE pages 334–335

_____ Concept Check: TE page 335

_____ Getting Ready to Practice Exercises: 1–9, SE page 336

APPLY/HOMEWORK

Homework Assignment

_____ Basic: Day 1: pp. 336–338 Exs. 10–20, 26–29, 34–39, 42–54, 58–70

_____ Average: Day 1: pp. 336–338 Exs. 14–25, 30–56, 60–65, 69–71

_____ Advanced: Day 1: pp. 336–338 Exs. 16–25, 32–57*, 60–65, 70, 71

Reteaching the Lesson

_____ Practice: CRB pages 32–34 (Level A, Level B, Level C); Practice Workbook

_____ Study Guide: CRB pages 35–36; Spanish Study Guide

Extending the Lesson

_____ Challenge: SE page 338; CRB page 37

ASSESSMENT OPTIONS

_____ Daily Homework Quiz (7.4): TE page 338 or Transparencies

_____ Test Taking Practice: SE page 338

Notes

_____

_____

Teacher's Name _____ Class _____ Room _____ Date _____

Lesson Plan for Block Scheduling

Half-block lesson (See *Pacing and Assignment Guide*, TE page 310A)

For use with pages 333–338

GOAL Use reciprocals to divide fractions.

State/Local Objectives _____

_____

✓ **Check the items you wish to use for this lesson.**

Chapter Pacing Guide	
Day	**Lesson**
1	7.1; 7.2 (begin)
2	7.2 (end); 7.3
3	**7.4**; 7.5
4	7.6; 7.7
5	Ch. 7 Review and Projects

STARTING OPTIONS

____ Homework Check (7.3): TE page 328; Answer Transparencies

____ Homework Quiz (7.3): TE page 330; Transparencies

____ Warm-Up: Transparencies

TEACHING OPTIONS

____ Notetaking Guide

____ Hands-on Activity: SE page 333

____ Examples: 1–3, SE pages 334–335

____ Extra Examples: TE page 335

____ Your Turn Now Exercises: 1–8, SE pages 334–335

____ Concept Check: TE page 335

____ Getting Ready to Practice Exercises: 1–9, SE page 336

APPLY/HOMEWORK

Homework Assignment

____ Block Schedule: pp. 336–338 Exs. 14–25, 30–56, 60–65, 69–71 (with 7.5)

Reteaching the Lesson

____ Practice: CRB pages 32–34 (Level A, Level B, Level C); Practice Workbook

____ Study Guide: CRB pages 35–36; Spanish Study Guide

Extending the Lesson

____ Challenge: SE page 338; CRB page 37

ASSESSMENT OPTIONS

____ Daily Homework Quiz (7.4): TE page 338 or Transparencies

____ Test Taking Practice: SE page 338

Notes

_____

_____

_____

Name _____ Date _____

Practice A

For use with pages 333–338

Tell whether the two numbers are reciprocals.

1. $\frac{3}{8}$ and $\frac{8}{3}$

2. $\frac{4}{5}$ and $\frac{5}{8}$

3. 3 and $\frac{1}{3}$

Write the reciprocal of the number.

4. $\frac{2}{3}$

5. $\frac{1}{9}$

6. 5

7. $\frac{7}{8}$

8. 4

9. $\frac{3}{10}$

Rewrite the division expression as an equivalent multiplication expression. Then evaluate the expression.

10. $\frac{1}{4} \div \frac{3}{8}$

11. $\frac{1}{6} \div \frac{2}{9}$

12. $8 \div \frac{12}{13}$

Find the quotient. Write the answer in simplest form.

13. $\frac{1}{2} \div \frac{5}{2}$

14. $\frac{3}{8} \div \frac{1}{4}$

15. $\frac{4}{5} \div \frac{3}{7}$

16. $\frac{10}{11} \div 5$

17. $6 \div \frac{20}{5}$

18. $\frac{2}{3} \div \frac{4}{9}$

19. $\frac{1}{12} \div \frac{1}{36}$

20. $\frac{8}{15} \div 4$

21. $7 \div \frac{5}{12}$

In Exercises 22–24, use the following information. You want to run a total of 8 miles over several days. You plan to run $\frac{2}{3}$ of a mile each day. How many days will it take you to run the 8 miles?

22. Write a division expression.

23. Use multiplication by the reciprocal to find the quotient.

24. Explain how to interpret the quotient to answer the question.

25. How many $\frac{1}{4}$ cups does it take to make 1 pint?
(*Hint:* 1 pint = 2 cups)

26. How many times does $\frac{1}{5}$ inch fit into $\frac{9}{10}$ inch?

LESSON
7.4

Name _____ Date _____

Practice B
For use with pages 333–338

Write the reciprocal of the number.

1. $\dfrac{1}{3}$

2. $\dfrac{4}{5}$

3. 7

4. $\dfrac{6}{11}$

5. 18

6. $\dfrac{2}{13}$

Complete the statement.

7. $\dfrac{3}{4} \times \underline{\ ?\ } = 1$

8. $\underline{\ ?\ } \times 5 = 1$

9. $\dfrac{7}{8} \times \dfrac{8}{7} = \underline{\ ?\ }$

10. $8 \div \dfrac{1}{3} = 8 \times \underline{\ ?\ } = \underline{\ ?\ }$

11. $10 \div \dfrac{1}{4} = \underline{\ ?\ } \times \underline{\ ?\ } = \underline{\ ?\ }$

Find the quotient. Write the answer in simplest form.

12. $\dfrac{1}{3} \div \dfrac{5}{6}$

13. $\dfrac{2}{5} \div \dfrac{8}{15}$

14. $8 \div \dfrac{4}{9}$

15. $\dfrac{24}{7} \div 4$

16. $\dfrac{5}{8} \div \dfrac{10}{3}$

17. $\dfrac{7}{12} \div \dfrac{3}{4}$

18. $\dfrac{12}{15} \div \dfrac{20}{27}$

19. $\dfrac{26}{55} \div \dfrac{34}{11}$

20. $15 \div \dfrac{3}{11}$

Evaluate the expression when $p = \frac{1}{4}$, $q = \frac{7}{8}$, and $r = 5$.

21. $p \div q$

22. $q \div r$

23. $q \div p$

24. $(r \div p) \div q$

25. $(q \div p) \div r$

26. $(p \div q) \div r$

27. How many times does $\frac{4}{7}$ inch fit into $\frac{12}{19}$ inch?

28. A person can type 15 words in $\frac{1}{4}$ of a minute. What is his average typing speed in words per minute?

29. A bakery makes 12 pies. The bakery sells the pies in pieces that are $\frac{1}{4}$ of the pie. How many pieces can they sell from the 12 pies? If they have 50 customers who want pie slices, will they have enough?

Lesson 7.4

Name _____ Date _____

Practice C

For use with pages 333–338

Write the reciprocal of the number.

1. $\dfrac{1}{4}$

2. $\dfrac{4}{7}$

3. 12

4. $\dfrac{5}{14}$

5. 3

6. $\dfrac{9}{13}$

Complete the statement.

7. $\dfrac{7}{9} \times \underline{\ ?\ } = 1$

8. $\underline{\ ?\ } \times 3 = 1$

9. $\dfrac{2}{11} \times \dfrac{11}{2} = \underline{\ ?\ }$

10. $6 \div \dfrac{1}{4} = 6 \times \underline{\ ?\ } = \underline{\ ?\ }$

11. $\dfrac{12}{17} \div \dfrac{4}{5} = \underline{\ ?\ } \times \underline{\ ?\ } = \underline{\ ?\ }$

Find the quotient. Write the answer in simplest form.

12. $\dfrac{9}{11} \div 3$

13. $\dfrac{4}{15} \div \dfrac{6}{11}$

14. $\dfrac{8}{9} \div \dfrac{4}{13}$

15. $12 \div \dfrac{2}{3}$

16. $\dfrac{7}{9} \div \dfrac{28}{54}$

17. $\dfrac{23}{25} \div 2$

18. $\dfrac{8}{13} \div \dfrac{3}{5}$

19. $\dfrac{1}{4} \div \dfrac{15}{16}$

20. $8 \div \dfrac{4}{15}$

21. $\dfrac{13}{15} \div \dfrac{5}{6}$

22. $\dfrac{11}{21} \div \dfrac{36}{35}$

23. $\dfrac{42}{56} \div \dfrac{81}{23}$

Evaluate the expression when $p = \frac{3}{5}$, $q = \frac{2}{9}$, and $r = 4$.

24. $p \div q$

25. $q \div r$

26. $q \div p$

27. $(r \div p) \div q$

28. $(q \div p) \div r$

29. $(p \div q) \div r$

Complete the statement using $<$, $>$, or $=$. Explain how you can determine the answer without actually finding the quotient.

30. $\dfrac{7}{12} \div 1 \underline{\ ?\ } \dfrac{7}{12}$

31. $5 \div \dfrac{1}{4} \underline{\ ?\ } 5$

32. $\dfrac{3}{8} \div 2 \underline{\ ?\ } \dfrac{3}{8}$

33. A typical adult has a resting heartrate of 12 beats per $\frac{1}{6}$ of a minute. How many beats per minute does this person have?

Name _____ Date _____

Study Guide

For use with pages 333–338

GOAL Use reciprocals to divide fractions.

VOCABULARY

Two numbers, such as $\frac{2}{9}$ and $\frac{9}{2}$, whose product is 1 are **reciprocals**.
Every number except 0 has a reciprocal. To find it, write the number as a fraction, and then switch the numerator and the denominator.

Rule for Dividing Fractions

Words To divide by a fraction, multiply by its reciprocal.

Numbers $\frac{3}{4} \div \frac{2}{5} = \frac{3}{4} \times \frac{5}{2}$ **Algebra** $\frac{x}{y} \div \frac{p}{q} = \frac{x}{y} \cdot \frac{q}{p}$

EXAMPLE 1 **Writing Reciprocals**

	Original Number	Fraction	Reciprocal	Check
a.	$\frac{2}{3}$	$\frac{2}{3}$	$\frac{3}{2}$	$\frac{2}{3} \cdot \frac{3}{2} = \frac{6}{6} = 1$
b.	9	$\frac{9}{1}$	$\frac{1}{9}$	$9 \times \frac{1}{9} = \frac{9}{9} = 1$
c.	$2\frac{3}{4}$	$\frac{11}{4}$	$\frac{4}{11}$	$\frac{11}{4} \cdot \frac{4}{11} = \frac{44}{44} = 1$

Exercises for Example 1

Write the reciprocal of the number.

1. $\frac{5}{6}$ **2.** $\frac{8}{5}$ **3.** 11   **4.** $1\frac{1}{2}$

EXAMPLE 2 **Dividing Two Fractions**

You walk $\frac{2}{3}$ mile in $\frac{1}{4}$ hour. Find your average walking rate in miles per hour.

Solution

Rate = Distance ÷ Time	Write the formula.
$= \frac{2}{3} \div \frac{1}{4}$	Use $\frac{2}{3}$ for the distance and $\frac{1}{4}$ for the time.
$= \frac{2}{3} \times \frac{4}{1}$	Multiply by the reciprocal of the divisor.
$= \frac{2 \times 4}{3 \times 1}$	Use the rule for multiplying fractions.
$= \frac{8}{3}$	Multiply.

Answer: Your average walking rate is $\frac{8}{3}$ miles per hour.

Lesson 7.4

Name _____ Date _____

Study Guide

For use with pages 333–338

Exercises for Example 2

Divide. Write the answer in simplest form.

5. $\dfrac{6}{7} \div \dfrac{1}{4}$ **6.** $\dfrac{2}{5} \div \dfrac{1}{2}$ **7.** $\dfrac{2}{3} \div \dfrac{1}{6}$ **8.** $\dfrac{3}{10} \div \dfrac{2}{5}$

EXAMPLE 3 Dividing a Fraction by a Whole Number

You have $\frac{2}{3}$ can of paint to paint 4 doors that are the same size.
How much paint can you use on each door?

Solution

$$\frac{2}{3} \div 4 = \frac{2}{3} \div \frac{4}{1}$$ Write 4 as an improper fraction.

$$= \frac{2}{3} \times \frac{1}{4}$$ Multiply by the reciprocal of the divisor.

$$= \frac{\overset{1}{2} \times 1}{3 \times \underset{2}{4}}$$ Use the rule for multiplying fractions.

$$= \frac{1}{6}$$ Multiply.

Answer: Each door gets $\frac{1}{6}$ can of paint.

EXAMPLE 4 Dividing a Whole Number by a Fraction

You are spray-painting patio chairs. You use $\frac{2}{3}$ can of spray-paint on each
chair. How many chairs can you cover with 4 cans of paint?

Solution

$$4 \div \frac{2}{3} = \frac{4}{1} \div \frac{2}{3}$$ Write 4 as an improper fraction.

$$= \frac{4}{1} \times \frac{3}{2}$$ Multiply by the reciprocal of the divisor.

$$= \frac{\overset{2}{4} \times 3}{1 \times \underset{1}{2}}$$ Use the rule for multiplying fractions.

$$= 6$$ Multiply.

Answer: You can paint 6 chairs.

Exercises for Examples 3 and 4

Divide. Write the answer in simplest form.

9. $\dfrac{3}{4} \div 5$ **10.** $\dfrac{5}{6} \div 4$ **11.** $6 \div \dfrac{3}{7}$

Lesson 7.4

Name _____ Date _____

Challenge Practice

For use with pages 333–338

Find the length of the rectangle with the given area.

1. Area = $\frac{3}{10}$ mm^2

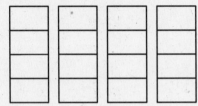

$\frac{2}{5}$ mm

?

2. Area = $\frac{1}{3}$ in.^{2}

$\frac{8}{21}$ in.

?

Write the division problem shown in the model.

3.

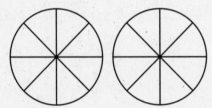

4.

In Exercises 5–8, evaluate the expression.

5. $\left(\frac{1}{2} - \frac{1}{3}\right) \div \frac{5}{8}$

6. $\left(\frac{1}{2} + \frac{1}{4}\right) \div \left(\frac{1}{2} + \frac{1}{3}\right)$

7. $\frac{7}{8} \div \frac{15}{16} \times \frac{5}{7}$

8. $\frac{2}{3} \times \left(\frac{7}{15} \div \frac{2}{5}\right)$

Teacher's Name _____ Class _____ Room _____ Date _____

Lesson Plan

1-day lesson (See *Pacing and Assignment Guide*, TE page 310A)

For use with pages 339–343

GOAL **Dividing mixed numbers.**

State/Local Objectives _____

_____

✓ Check the items you wish to use for this lesson.

STARTING OPTIONS

____ Homework Check (7.4): TE page 336; Answer Transparencies

____ Homework Quiz (7.4): TE page 338; Transparencies

____ Warm-Up: Transparencies

TEACHING OPTIONS

____ Notetaking Guide

____ Examples: 1–3, SE pages 339–340

____ Extra Examples: TE page 340

____ Your Turn Now Exercises: 1–5, SE page 340

____ Technology Activity with Keystrokes: CRB pages 40–41

____ Activity Master: CRB page 42

____ Concept Check: TE page 340

____ Getting Ready to Practice Exercises: 1–6, SE page 341

APPLY/HOMEWORK

Homework Assignment

____ Basic: Day 1: pp. 341–343 Exs. 7–15, 22–29, 32–37, 39–45, 50–57

____ Average: Day 1: pp. 341–343 Exs. 7–17, 22–25, 30–48, 50–52, 56–58

____ Advanced: Day 1: pp. 341–343 Exs. 7–11, 18–25, 28–51*, 56–58

Reteaching the Lesson

____ Practice: CRB pages 43–45 (Level A, Level B, Level C); Practice Workbook

____ Study Guide: CRB pages 46–47; Spanish Study Guide

Extending the Lesson

____ Real-World Problem Solving: CRB page 48

____ Challenge: SE page 343; CRB page 49

ASSESSMENT OPTIONS

____ Daily Homework Quiz (7.5): TE page 343 or Transparencies

____ Test Taking Practice: SE page 343

Notes

_____

Teacher's Name _____ Class _____ Room _____ Date _____

Lesson Plan for Block Scheduling

Half-block lesson (See *Pacing and Assignment*, TE page 310A)

For use with pages 339–343

GOAL **Dividing mixed numbers.**

State/Local Objectives _____

_____

✓ Check the items you wish to use for this lesson.

Chapter Pacing Guide	
Day	**Lesson**
1	7.1; 7.2 (begin)
2	7.2 (end); 7.3
3	7.4; **7.5**
4	7.6; 7.7
5	Ch. 7 Review and Projects

STARTING OPTIONS

____ Homework Check (7.4): TE page 336; Answer Transparencies

____ Homework Quiz (7.4): TE page 338; Transparencies

____ Warm-Up: Transparencies

TEACHING OPTIONS

____ Notetaking Guide

____ Examples: 1–3, SE pages 339–340

____ Extra Examples: TE page 340

____ Your Turn Now Exercises: 1–5, SE page 340

____ Technology Activity with Keystrokes: CRB pages 40–41

____ Activity Master: CRB page 42

____ Concept Check: TE page 340

____ Getting Ready to Practice Exercises: 1–6, SE page 341

APPLY/HOMEWORK

Homework Assignment

____ Block Schedule: pp. 341–343 Exs. 7–17, 22–25, 30–48, 50–52, 56–58 (with 7.4)

Reteaching the Lesson

____ Practice: CRB pages 43–45 (Level A, Level B, Level C); Practice Workbook

____ Study Guide: CRB pages 46–47; Spanish Study Guide

Extending the Lesson

____ Real-World Problem Solving: CRB page 48

____ Challenge: SE page 343; CRB page 49

ASSESSMENT OPTIONS

____ Daily Homework Quiz (7.5): TE page 343 or Transparencies

____ Test Taking Practice: SE page 343

Notes

_____

_____

LESSON 7.5

Technology Activity

For use with pages 339–343

GOAL Use a calculator to divide mixed numbers.

EXAMPLE A $9\frac{1}{2}$-minute shower used $23\frac{3}{4}$ gallons of water. Find the number of gallons of water used per minute. Write your answer as a mixed number.

Solution

To find the number of gallons of water used per minute, you must divide the number of gallons of water by the number of minutes.

Keystrokes   **Display**

23 UNIT 3 / 4 ÷ 9 UNIT 1 / 2 = $\boxed{2 \llcorner 1/2}$

Answer: The number of gallons of water used per minute is $2\frac{1}{2}$.

Your turn now **Use a calculator to evaluate the expression. Write your answer as a mixed number.**

1. $11\frac{1}{2} \div 5\frac{1}{4}$ **2.** $15\frac{5}{6} \div 12\frac{2}{9}$ **3.** $20\frac{4}{7} \div 5\frac{1}{3}$

4. $25\frac{5}{6} \div 10\frac{1}{3}$ **5.** $24\frac{2}{5} \div 9\frac{5}{7}$ **6.** $29\frac{4}{9} \div 4\frac{1}{6}$

7. $30\frac{6}{7} \div 9\frac{1}{7}$ **8.** $22\frac{2}{3} \div 2\frac{1}{8}$ **9.** $26\frac{8}{9} \div 10\frac{4}{7}$

10. $7\frac{3}{8} \times 3\frac{1}{4} \div 2\frac{5}{6}$ **11.** $10\frac{7}{9} \div 2\frac{4}{5} \times 8\frac{2}{3}$ **12.** $30\frac{2}{3} \times 6\frac{4}{7} \div 2\frac{2}{5}$

Choose the correct operation. Then solve.

13. On a 56-mile trip, a car uses $2\frac{3}{4}$ gallons of gas. Find the number of miles traveled per gallon of gasoline.

14. A showerhead uses $2\frac{1}{2}$ gallons per minute. Find how many gallons of water are used for a shower that takes 11 minutes.

15. A box of raisins weighs 16 ounces. If one serving of raisins is $1\frac{2}{5}$ ounces, how many servings of raisins are in the box?

16. You have two cats. The total amount of cat food the cats eat each day is $1\frac{1}{3}$ cups. If you can feed your cats for 21 days from a medium-sized bag, how many cups of cat food does the bag contain?

LESSON 7.5

Name _____ Date _____

Technology Activity Keystrokes

For use with Technology Activity on page 40

TI-34 II

23 [UNIT] 3 [/] 4 [÷] 9 [UNIT] 1 [/] 2 [ENTER]

TI-73

22 [UNIT] 3 [▼] 4 [▶] [÷] 9 [UNIT] 1 [▼] 2 [ENTER]

7.5 Activity Master

For use before Lesson 7.5

Goal
Find the quotient of two mixed numbers using measuring cups.

Materials
- measuring cup
- large bowl
- pencil and paper
- popcorn kernels

Dividing Mixed Numbers

In this activity, you will divide mixed numbers using a measuring cup.

EXPLORE Find the quotient of $3\frac{3}{4}$ and $1\frac{1}{4}$.

❶ Use the measuring cup to put $3\frac{3}{4}$ cups of popcorn kernels into the large bowl.

❷ Use the measuring cup to remove $1\frac{1}{4}$ cups of kernels from the bowl. Make a tally mark on a piece of paper.

❸ Repeat step 2 as many times as it takes to empty the bowl. When the bowl is empty, count the number of tally marks you have. That number is the quotient of $3\frac{3}{4}$ and $1\frac{1}{4}$.

your turn now

1. Rewrite each dividend and divisor as improper fractions to complete column 2 of the table.

	Write as improper fractions	Quotient (Number of tally marks)
$3\frac{3}{4} \div 1\frac{1}{4}$	$\underline{\ ?\ } \div \underline{\ ?\ }$	$\underline{\ ?\ }$
$6 \div 1\frac{1}{2}$	$\underline{\ ?\ } \div \underline{\ ?\ }$	$\underline{\ ?\ }$
$6\frac{1}{4} \div 1\frac{1}{4}$	$\underline{\ ?\ } \div \underline{\ ?\ }$	$\underline{\ ?\ }$
$5\frac{1}{3} \div 2\frac{2}{3}$	$\underline{\ ?\ } \div \underline{\ ?\ }$	$\underline{\ ?\ }$

2. Use the process with the measuring cup to find the quotients in column 3 of the table.

3. Look at the second and third columns of your table. Can you find a shortcut for dividing mixed numbers with the same denominator? If so, describe it.

Name _____ Date _____

7.5 Practice A

For use with pages 339–343

Match the number to its reciprocal.

1. $2\frac{1}{3}$

A. $\frac{6}{25}$

2. $4\frac{1}{6}$

B. $\frac{3}{13}$

3. $3\frac{2}{3}$

C. $\frac{3}{7}$

4. $2\frac{5}{6}$

D. $\frac{3}{11}$

5. $4\frac{1}{3}$

E. $\frac{6}{17}$

6. Are $2\frac{2}{3}$ and $3\frac{3}{2}$ reciprocals? Why or why not?

Write the reciprocal of the divisor. Then find the quotient. Use estimation to check your answer.

7. $2\frac{4}{5} \div \frac{9}{10}$

8. $4\frac{1}{3} \div 9\frac{5}{6}$

9. $\frac{7}{9} \div 6\frac{2}{5}$

Find the quotient. Write the answer in simplest form.

10. $4\frac{1}{8} \div \frac{5}{8}$

11. $7\frac{3}{5} \div \frac{4}{5}$

12. $3\frac{6}{11} \div 8$

13. $6\frac{7}{12} \div 5$

14. $\frac{3}{7} \div 3\frac{1}{4}$

15. $\frac{11}{12} \div 2\frac{4}{9}$

16. $12 \div 3\frac{3}{8}$

17. $10 \div 4\frac{1}{4}$

18. $3\frac{1}{3} \div 2\frac{1}{2}$

19. A golf ball display case is 19 inches wide. A golf ball is $1\frac{1}{8}$ inches wide. How many golf balls can you display in your case?

20. Jim earned $25\frac{1}{2}$ dollars at work last week. His wage is $5\frac{1}{4}$ dollars an hour. How many hours did Jim work last week?

LESSON 7.5

Practice B

For use with pages 339–343

Name _____ Date _____

1. What division problem involving a mixed number is represented by the model? What is the quotient?

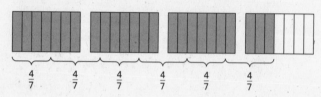

$$\frac{4}{7} \quad \frac{4}{7} \quad \frac{4}{7} \quad \frac{4}{7} \quad \frac{4}{7} \quad \frac{4}{7}$$

Find the quotient. Write the answer in simplest form.

2. $2\frac{1}{4} \div \frac{3}{4}$

3. $8\frac{7}{10} \div \frac{3}{20}$

4. $10\frac{2}{7} \div 6$

5. $3\frac{12}{13} \div \frac{5}{11}$

6. $\frac{8}{15} \div 6\frac{2}{5}$

7. $9 \div 10\frac{4}{5}$

8. $6\frac{1}{2} \div 5\frac{1}{8}$

9. $4\frac{1}{3} \div 2\frac{1}{4}$

10. $5\frac{5}{6} \div 3\frac{2}{9}$

Solve. Explain why you chose the operation you used.

11. Tom played 9 holes in a round of golf. He shot par on $\frac{2}{3}$ of the holes. On how many holes did he make par?

12. Carlos went to the grocery store and purchased $1\frac{3}{5}$ pounds of red apples and $2\frac{1}{4}$ pounds of green apples. How many pounds of apples did he buy?

13. You need to make 6 phone calls. Each phone call will last $3\frac{5}{9}$ minutes. How long will you be on the phone to make all of the phone calls?

14. You need $2\frac{1}{2}$ cups of flour for a recipe, but you only have a $\frac{1}{3}$ measuring cup. How many times will you need to use the measuring cup to get the full amount?

Estimate the quotient.

15. $15\frac{4}{5} \div 4\frac{1}{8}$

16. $20\frac{1}{9} \div 4\frac{9}{10}$

17. $22 \div 1\frac{6}{7}$

Practice C

For use with pages 339–343

Find the quotient. Write the answer in simplest form.

1. $3\frac{4}{7} \div \frac{5}{7}$

2. $12\frac{1}{4} \div \frac{11}{12}$

3. $6\frac{5}{8} \div 3$

4. $4\frac{5}{9} \div \frac{2}{3}$

5. $\frac{8}{15} \div 2\frac{3}{5}$

6. $10 \div 3\frac{2}{7}$

7. $14\frac{2}{3} \div 3\frac{5}{9}$

8. $20\frac{6}{13} \div 6\frac{8}{15}$

9. $16\frac{8}{21} \div 5\frac{1}{3}$

10. A container of laundry soap has $2\frac{19}{20}$ liters of soap. If you are able to do 26 loads of laundry, how much soap do you put into each load of laundry?

11. You have a bookshelf that is $15\frac{5}{12}$ inches long. Each book is $2\frac{1}{4}$ inches thick. How many books will you be able to fit on the bookshelf?

Evaluate the expression.

12. $2\frac{1}{2} \div \frac{5}{16} \times 2\frac{2}{3}$

13. $9\frac{1}{6} \div 2\frac{1}{12} + \frac{3}{5}$

14. $3\frac{11}{12} \div 2 - \frac{7}{8}$

In Exercises 15–17, use the following information. A builder is constructing a house that is 40 feet long. A stud is a wood board used as an upright support in the framework to build a wall. He needs to put studs every $1\frac{1}{3}$ feet.

15. Write an expression that represents the number of studs the builder will need to put into the 40 foot wall.

16. Use a pair of compatible numbers to estimate the value of the expression you wrote in Exercise 15.

17. How many studs should be used on the wall?

Evaluate the expression when $x = \frac{3}{5}$ and $y = 2\frac{1}{2}$.

18. $\frac{3x}{y}$

19. $y + \frac{4}{x}$

20. $\frac{x}{y-1}$

LESSON 7.5

Study Guide

For use with pages 339–343

GOAL Divide mixed numbers.

EXAMPLE 1 Dividing a Mixed Number

a. $4\frac{1}{2} \div \frac{3}{4} = \frac{9}{2} \div \frac{3}{4}$ Write $4\frac{1}{2}$ as an improper fraction.

$= \frac{9}{2} \times \frac{4}{3}$ Multiply by the reciprocal of the divisor.

$= \frac{\overset{3}{9} \times \overset{2}{4}}{\underset{1}{2} \times \underset{1}{3}}$ Use the rule for multiplying fractions. Divide out common factors.

$= 6$ Multiply.

b. $6\frac{2}{3} \div 5 = \frac{20}{3} \div \frac{5}{1}$ Write $6\frac{2}{3}$ and 5 as improper fractions.

$= \frac{20}{3} \times \frac{1}{5}$ Multiply by the reciprocal of the divisor.

$= \frac{\overset{4}{20} \times 1}{3 \times \underset{1}{5}}$ Use the rule for multiplying fractions. Divide out common factors.

$= \frac{4}{3}$ Multiply.

Exercises for Example 1

Divide.

1. $3\frac{2}{3} \div \frac{1}{6}$
2. $2\frac{1}{2} \div \frac{2}{3}$
3. $5\frac{1}{4} \div \frac{3}{2}$
4. $7\frac{1}{2} \div \frac{3}{4}$

5. $4\frac{1}{5} \div 7$
6. $2\frac{1}{4} \div 3$
7. $2\frac{1}{2} \div 5$
8. $5\frac{1}{3} \div 4$

EXAMPLE 2 Dividing by a Mixed Number

$8\frac{3}{4} \div 2\frac{1}{2} = \frac{35}{4} \div \frac{5}{2}$ Write $8\frac{3}{4}$ and $2\frac{1}{2}$ as improper fractions.

$= \frac{35}{4} \times \frac{2}{5}$ Multiply by the reciprocal of the divisor.

$= \frac{\overset{7}{35} \times \overset{1}{2}}{\underset{2}{4} \times \underset{1}{5}}$ Use the rule for multiplying fractions. Divide out common factors.

$= \frac{7}{2}$, or $3\frac{1}{2}$ Multiply.

✓ **Check:** Round $8\frac{3}{4}$ to 9 and replace $2\frac{1}{2}$ with the compatible number 3.

The answer is reasonable because it is close to the estimate $9 \div 3 = 3$.

LESSON 7.5 Continued

Study Guide
For use with pages 339–343

Exercises for Example 2

Divide. Use estimation to check your answer.

9. $6 \div 3\frac{1}{3}$ **10.** $8 \div 2\frac{3}{4}$ **11.** $4 \div 3\frac{1}{2}$ **12.** $6 \div 5\frac{1}{3}$

13. $2\frac{1}{2} \div 3\frac{1}{3}$ **14.** $4\frac{1}{2} \div 1\frac{1}{4}$ **15.** $3\frac{1}{4} \div 2\frac{1}{2}$ **16.** $2\frac{1}{5} \div 1\frac{1}{5}$

EXAMPLE 3 **Choosing an Operation**

You need $6\frac{3}{4}$ cups of flour to make 3 batches of cookies. About how many cups of flour do you need to make 1 batch of cookies?

Solution

(1) Choose the operation by thinking about a similar whole number problem: If 6 cups of flour made 3 batches of cookies, you would *divide* 6 by 3. So, *divide* $6\frac{3}{4}$ by 3.

(2) Divide. $6\frac{3}{4} \div 3 = \frac{27}{4} \div \frac{3}{1}$

$$= \frac{27}{4} \times \frac{1}{3}$$

$$= \frac{\overset{9}{\cancel{27}} \times 1}{4 \times \underset{1}{\cancel{3}}}$$

$$= \frac{9}{4}, \text{ or } 2\frac{1}{4}$$

Answer: You need $2\frac{1}{4}$ cups of flour to make 1 batch of cookies.

Exercises for Example 3

17. You have a $1\frac{1}{2}$ gallon bucket. How many times must you fill the bucket if you need 9 gallons of water?

18. You need $1\frac{1}{4}$ cups of sugar to make a batch of cookies. How many cups of sugar do you need to make $\frac{1}{2}$ batch of cookies?

Name _____ Date _____

Real-World Problem Solving

For use with pages 339–343

Real Estate

Savings accounts, stocks, bonds, and collectibles are some of the things you can invest your money in. Another is real estate. Real estate is property that can be owned, such as land or buildings. The value of real estate tends to increase over time. The value can also be affected by factors like the condition, location, and type of property. Businesses may pay more for a property in a busy area. A well-maintained home or building is worth more than one in need of repair. A large piece of land may sell for more if subdivided into smaller lots that are sold individually to build houses on. Investing in real estate is a little riskier than placing your money in a savings account, but the money you get back in the end is often greater.

In Exercises 1–3, use the following information.

Several years ago, Ricardo Lucia purchased 50 acres of land. The value had increased, so he decided to sell the land. A contractor named Janet Hall bought the land to build new homes on it. Each home is to be built on a separate lot. Janet is considering what size the lots should be. She sells each lot for a set price, then charges another price for building the house. Larger lots can be sold for more money, but if the land is divided into smaller lots, there are more to sell.

1. How many $\frac{1}{2}$ acre lots can Janet get from the land? How many $1\frac{1}{2}$ acre lots? How many $1\frac{3}{4}$ acre lots?

2. Janet wants to receive a total of $500,000 for the land. If she decides to go with the $\frac{1}{2}$ acre lots, how much should she charge for each lot?

3. If Janet were to use $1\frac{1}{4}$ acre lots, how much would she need to charge for each lot?

Name _____ Date _____

Challenge Practice

For use with pages 339–343

1. One pound of brown sugar is equivalent to $2\frac{1}{4}$ cups of firmly packed brown sugar. A recipe for chocolate chip cookies requires $\frac{3}{4}$ cup of firmly packed brown sugar. You have $1\frac{2}{3}$ pounds of brown sugar available. How many batches of chocolate chip cookies could you make?

In Exercises 2–4, use the table below that shows the long jump distances for college men and women who were trying to qualify for the olympic games.

Men	Distance (in feet)	Women	Distance (in feet)
25 ft $3\frac{1}{2}$ in.		19 ft $6\frac{3}{4}$ in.	
23 ft $5\frac{1}{4}$ in.		18 ft $9\frac{3}{4}$ in.	
22 ft $1\frac{1}{2}$ in.		18 ft $7\frac{3}{4}$ in.	
21 ft $8\frac{3}{4}$ in.		18 ft $6\frac{1}{2}$ in.	
21 ft 6 in.		18 ft 3 in.	

2. Complete each long jump distance as a mixed number of feet.
   (*Hint:* 1 foot = 12 inches)

3. What is the average (mean) distance for the men's long jump?

4. What is the average (mean) distance for the women's long jump?

LESSON 7.6

Lesson Plan

1-day lesson (See *Pacing and Assignment Guide*, TE page 310A)

For use with pages 344–347

GOAL Use customary units of weight and capacity.

State/Local Objectives _____

_____

Lesson 7.6

✓ **Check the items you wish to use for this lesson.**

STARTING OPTIONS

_____ Homework Check (7.5): TE page 341; Answer Transparencies

_____ Homework Quiz (7.5): TE page 343; Transparencies

_____ Warm-Up: Transparencies

TEACHING OPTIONS

_____ Notetaking Guide

_____ Examples: 1–3, SE pages 344–345

_____ Extra Examples: TE page 345

_____ Your Turn Now Exercises: 1–6, SE pages 344–345

_____ Concept Check: TE page 345

_____ Getting Ready to Practice Exercises: 1–6, SE page 346

APPLY/HOMEWORK

Homework Assignment

_____ Basic: Day 1: EP p. 711 Exs. 36–41; pp. 346–347 Exs. 7–20, 24–27, 31–41

_____ Average: Day 1: pp. 346–347 Exs. 7–17, 21–29, 31–42

_____ Advanced: Day 1: pp. 346–347 Exs. 7–17, 21–35*, 40–42

Reteaching the Lesson

_____ Practice: CRB pages 52–54 (Level A, Level B, Level C); Practice Workbook

_____ Study Guide: CRB pages 55–56; Spanish Study Guide

Extending the Lesson

_____ Challenge: SE page 347; CRB page 57

ASSESSMENT OPTIONS

_____ Daily Quiz (2.6): TE page 347 or Transparencies

_____ Test Taking Practice: SE page 347

Notes _____

_____

_____

LESSON 7.6

Lesson Plan for Block Scheduling

Half-block lesson (See *Pacing and Assignment Guide*, TE page 310A)

For use with pages 344–347

GOAL   Use customary units of weight and capacity.

State/Local Objectives _____

_____

✓ **Check the items you wish to use for this lesson.**

Chapter Pacing Guide	
Day	**Lesson**
1	7.1; 7.2 (begin)
2	7.2 (end); 7.3
3	7.4; 7.5
4	**7.6**; 7.7
5	Ch. 7 Review and Projects

Lesson 7.6

STARTING OPTIONS

____ Homework Check (7.5): TE page 341; Answer Transparencies

____ Homework Quiz (7.5): TE page 343; Transparencies

____ Warm-Up: Transparencies

TEACHING OPTIONS

____ Notetaking Guide

____ Examples: 1–3, SE pages 344–345

____ Extra Examples: TE page 345

____ Your Turn Now Exercises: 1–6, SE pages 344–345

____ Concept Check: TE page 345

____ Getting Ready to Practice Exercises: 1–6, SE page 346

APPLY/HOMEWORK

Homework Assignment

____ Block Schedule: pp. 346–347 Exs. 7–17, 21–29, 31–42 (with 7.7)

Reteaching the Lesson

____ Practice: CRB pages 52–54 (Level A, Level B, Level C); Practice Workbook

____ Study Guide: CRB pages 55–56; Spanish Study Guide

Extending the Lesson

____ Challenge: SE page 347; CRB page 57

ASSESSMENT OPTIONS

____ Daily Quiz (2.6): TE page 347 or Transparencies

____ Test Taking Practice: SE page 347

Notes _____

_____

_____

_____

LESSON 7.6

Practice A

For use with pages 344–347

Choose an appropriate customary unit to measure the item.

1. weight of a tennis ball

2. capacity of a tea cup

3. capacity of a kitchen sink

4. weight of an elephant

Complete the statement using *fluid ounces*, *pints*, or *gallons*.

5. The capacity of a glass of water is 8 __?__.

6. The amount of water in a water cooler is 10 __?__.

7. The amount of ice cream in a box is 8 __?__.

8. The amount of laundry soap in a prepackaged dispenser is 100 __?__.

Tell whether the measurement is a *weight*, a *capacity*, or a *length*.

9. 4 pints

10. $1\frac{2}{3}$ inches

11. 7 ounces

12. $2\frac{5}{7}$ fluid ounces

13. 15 quarts

14. $6\frac{1}{8}$ feet

Complete the statement.

15. 1 c = __?__ fl oz

16. 1 gal = __?__ qt

17. 6000 lb = __?__ T

18. 5 gal = __?__ qt

19. 4 c = __?__ pt

20. 2 lb = __?__ oz

Choose the list that puts the units in *increasing* order.

21. **A.** pound, ounce, ton

    C. ton, pound, ounce

    B. ounce, pound, ton

    D. ton, ounce, pound

22. **A.** gallon, cup, pint, quart

    C. quart, cup, pint, gallon

    B. cup, quart, pint, gallon

    D. cup, pint, quart, gallon

23. Clarice measured the capacity of a pitcher of water to be 64; however, she can't remember the units that she measured it in. Should the units be gallons, fluid ounces, or cups?

24. Tony needs to determine the weight of his car. What customary units should he use to measure the car: ounces, tons, or pounds?

25. You fill a glass with 2 cups of milk. How many fluid ounces of milk do you put into the glass?

Lesson 7.6

Name _____ Date _____

Practice B
For use with pages 344–347

Choose an appropriate customary unit to measure the item.

1. weight of a horse

2. capacity of a teapot

3. capacity of an eyedropper

4. weight of a potato

5. weight of a person

6. capacity of a swimming pool

Complete the statement using *fluid ounces*, *pints*, or *gallons*.

7. The capacity of an orange juice jug is $\frac{3}{4}$ __?__ .

8. The amount of yogurt in a container is 6 __?__ .

9. The amount of salad dressing in a container is 1 __?__ .

10. The amount of coffee a coffee maker makes is 6 __?__ .

Tell whether the measurement is a *weight*, a *capacity*, or a *length*.

11. 2 inches

12. $7\frac{4}{5}$ fluid ounces

13. 2 ounces

14. $14\frac{3}{10}$ gallons

15. 12 feet

16. $3\frac{1}{4}$ tons

Complete the statement.

17. 1 lb = __?__ oz

18. 4 qt = __?__ gal

19. 16 c = __?__ pt

20. 4 qt = __?__ pt

21. 8000 lb = __?__ T

22. 2 gal = __?__ qt

Choose the best estimate for the weight of the object.

23. adult female Bengal tiger

    A. 30 oz   **B.** 30 T   **C.** 300 lb   **D.** 300 oz

24. semi-truck

    A. 20 oz   **B.** 20 T   **C.** 20 lb   **D.** 200 oz

25. apple

    A. $6\frac{1}{4}$ T   **B.** $6\frac{1}{4}$ lb   **C.** $6\frac{1}{4}$ oz   **D.** $60\frac{1}{4}$ oz

26. A chef has 48 fluid ounces of milk and uses it in 12 different batches of pancakes. How many ounces of milk does each batch get?

Name _____ Date _____

7.6 Practice C

For use with pages 344–347

Choose an appropriate customary unit to measure the item.

1. weight of a fly

2. capacity of a trash can

3. capacity of a medicine dropper

4. weight of an apple

5. weight of a hippopotamus

6. capacity of a bath tub

7. Which unit is used for the *largest* weight?

   A. tons   **B.** pounds   **C.** ounces

8. Which unit is used for the *smallest* capacity?

   A. cups   **B.** pints   **C.** gallons   **D.** fluid ounces

Tell whether the measurement is a *weight*, a *capacity*, or a *length*.

9. 16 pounds

10. 4 inches

11. $2\frac{3}{4}$ cups

12. $8\frac{1}{2}$ ounces

13. 9 pints

14. 7 gallons

Complete the statement.

15. 48 oz = __?__ lb

16. 5 c = __?__ fl oz

17. 8 pt = __?__ qt

18. 3 T = __?__ lb

19. 1 gal = __?__ qt = __?__ pt = __?__ c

20. 16 pt = __?__ qt = __?__ gal

Choose an appropriate customary unit to measure the weight of the item.

21. bag of onions

22. train engine

23. cotton ball

24. pencil

25. In a metal factory, a machinist measures out 1 pound of aluminum and 1 pound of steel. Which of the metals do you think has the larger volume? Explain.

Tell whether the given object has a capacity that is *less than a pint*, about *equal to a pint*, or *more than a pint*.

26. bucket

27. drinking glass

28. lake

29. laundry basket

30. eyedropper

31. large mug

Name _____ Date _____

Study Guide

For use with pages 344–347

GOAL Use customary units of weight and capacity.

VOCABULARY

Three customary units of weight are the **ounce** (oz), the **pound** (lb), and the **ton** (T).

Benchmarks An **ounce** is about the weight of a slice of bread. A **pound** is about the weight of a soccer ball. A **ton** is about the weight of a compact car.

Ounces, pounds, and tons are related to each other.

$$1 \text{ lb} = 16 \text{ oz} \qquad 1 \text{ T} = 2000 \text{ lb}$$

Five customary units of capacity are the **fluid ounce** (fl oz), the **cup** (c), the **pint** (pt), the **quart** (qt), and the **gallon** (gal). The units of capacity are related to each other.

$$1 \text{ c} = 8 \text{ fl oz} \qquad 1 \text{ pt} = 2 \text{ c} \qquad 1 \text{ qt} = 2 \text{ pt} \qquad 1 \text{ gal} = 4 \text{ qt}$$

EXAMPLE 1 **Choosing Units of Weight**

Choose the appropriate customary unit of weight.

a. A tennis ball weighs 2 __?__ .

b. A pickup truck weights 2 __?__ .

Solution

a. A tennis ball weighs 2 *ounces*, because it is heavier than a slice of bread and lighter than a soccer ball.

b. A pickup truck weighs 2 *tons*, because it is heavier than a compact car.

Exercises for Example 1

Choose an appropriate customary unit to measure the weight of the item.

1. football

2. elephant

3. kiwi fruit

LESSON 7.6 Continued

Name _____ Date _____

Study Guide

For use with pages 344–347

Lesson 7.6

EXAMPLE 2 **Choosing Units of Capacity**

Choose an appropriate customary unit to measure the capacity.

   a. wheelbarrow   **b.** small saucepan

Solution

   a. A wheelbarrow holds much more than a gallon. You can use gallons, but you wouldn't use the smaller units.

   b. A small saucepan holds less than a gallon. You can use quarts or one of the smaller units, pints or cups.

Exercises for Example 2

Choose an appropriate customary unit to measure the capacity.

   4. yogurt container

   5. laundry tub

   6. soup spoon

EXAMPLE 3 **Choosing Customary Units**

What does each measure describe about an empty ceramic flower vase?

   a. 2 lb   **b.** 2 qt

Solution

   a. A pound is a measure of weight, so 2 pounds describes how much the empty vase weighs.

   b. A quart is a measure of capacity, so 2 quarts describes the amount of water the vase can hold.

Exercises for Example 3

Choose an appropriate customary unit to measure.

   7. weight of a pet cat

   8. capacity of a gasoline can

   9. weight of a DVD disc

Middle School Math, Course 1
Chapter 7   Resource Book

In Exercises 1–5, use the clues to guess the object being described.

1. I weigh less than one pound.

   I am about the size of a person's fist.

   I pump $5\frac{1}{4}$ quarts of blood every minute.

   What am I?

2. I am used to measure small amounts of ingredients in a recipe.

   It takes 16 of me to fill one cup.

   There are 8 of me in one stick of butter.

   What am I?

3. I am an appliance that has a water capacity of 15 gallons.

   I use about 4 ounces of soap.

   I can clean about 18 pounds of dirty items.

   What am I?

4. I am an animal that weighs about 6 tons.

   I eat about 300 pounds of food a day.

   I drink up to 40 gallons of water a day.

   What am I?

5. I weigh about 2 tons.

   I can carry about $\frac{3}{4}$ ton.

   My tank hold 26 gallons.

   What am I?

Lesson 7.6

Teacher's Name _____ Class _____ Room _____ Date _____

Lesson Plan

LESSON 7.7

1-day lesson (See *Pacing and Assignment Guide*, TE page 310A)

For use with pages 348-355

GOAL Change customary units of measure.

State/Local Objectives _____

_____

✓ Check the items you wish to use for this lesson.

STARTING OPTIONS

_____ Homework Check (7.6): TE page 346; Answer Transparencies

_____ Homework Quiz (7.6): TE page 347; Transparencies

_____ Warm-Up: Transparencies

TEACHING OPTIONS

_____ Notetaking Guide

_____ Examples: 1–5, SE pages 350–352

_____ Extra Examples: TE pages 351–352

_____ Your Turn Now Exercises: 1–6, SE pages 350–351

_____ Technology Keystrokes for Technology Activity on SE page 355: CRB page 60

_____ Technology Keystrokes for Exs. 40 and 49 on SE pages 353 and 354: CRB page 61

_____ Concept Check: TE page 352

_____ Getting Ready to Practice Exercises: 1–11, SE page 352

APPLY/HOMEWORK

Homework Assignment

_____ Basic: Day 1: SRH p. 701 Exs. 1–6; pp. 353–354 Exs. 12–21, 28–31, 33–44, 50–60

_____ Average: Day 1: pp. 353–354 Exs. 15–24, 28–35, 39–48, 50–55, 59–61

_____ Advanced: Day 1: pp. 353–354 Exs. 15–21, 25–32, 36–41, 45–55*, 60, 61

Reteaching the Lesson

_____ Practice: CRB pages 62–64 (Level A, Level B, Level C); Practice Workbook

_____ Study Guide: CRB pages 65–66; Spanish Study Guide

Extending the Lesson

_____ Real-World Problem Solving: CRB page 67

_____ Challenge: SE page 354; CRB page 68

ASSESSMENT OPTIONS

_____ Daily Quiz (7.7): TE page 354 or Transparencies

_____ Test Taking Practice: SE page 354

_____ Quiz (7.4–7.7): SE page 357; Assessment Book page 80

Notes _____

58 **Middle School Math, Course 1**
Chapter 7   Resource Book

Teacher's Name _____ **Class** _____ **Room** _____ **Date** _____

LESSON 7.7

Lesson Plan for Block Scheduling

Half-block lesson (See *Pacing and Assignment Guide*, TE page 310A)

For use with pages 348–355

GOAL Change customary units of measure.

State/Local Objectives _____

_____

✓ Check the items you wish to use for this lesson.

Chapter Pacing Guide	
Day	**Lesson**
1	7.1; 7.2 (begin)
2	7.2 (end); 7.3
3	7.4; 7.5
4	7.6; **7.7**
5	Ch. 7 Review and Projects

STARTING OPTIONS

____ Homework Check (7.6): TE page 346; Answer Transparencies

____ Homework Quiz (7.6): TE page 347; Transparencies

____ Warm-Up: Transparencies

TEACHING OPTIONS

____ Notetaking Guide

____ Examples: 1–5, SE pages 350–352

____ Extra Examples: TE pages 351–352

____ Your Turn Now Exercises: 1–6, SE pages 350–351

____ Technology Keystrokes for Technology Activity on SE page 355: CRB page 60

____ Technology Keystrokes for Exs. 40 and 49 on SE pages 353 and 354: CRB page 61

____ Concept Check: TE page 352

____ Getting Ready to Practice Exercises: 1–11, SE page 352

APPLY/HOMEWORK

Homework Assignment

____ Block Schedule: pp. 353–354 Exs. 15–24, 28–35, 39–48, 50–55, 59–61 (with 7.6)

Reteaching the Lesson

____ Practice: CRB pages 62–64 (Level A, Level B, Level C); Practice Workbook

____ Study Guide: CRB pages 65–66; Spanish Study Guide

Extending the Lesson

____ Real-World Problem Solving: CRB page 67

____ Challenge: SE page 354; CRB page 68

ASSESSMENT OPTIONS

____ Daily Quiz (7.7): TE page 354 or Transparencies

____ Test Taking Practice: SE page 354

____ Quiz (7.4–7.7): SE page 357; Assessment Book page 80

Notes _____

_____

Lesson 7.7

Technology Activity Keystrokes

For use with Technology Activity 7.7, page 355

TI-34 II

0.621 [STO▸] [ENTER=]

340 [×] [2nd] [RCL] [ENTER=] [ENTER=]

TI-73

0.621 [STO▸] [2nd] [TEXT] [ENTER] [▼] [▼] [▼] [▼] [ENTER] [ENTER]

340 [×] [2nd] [RCL] [2nd] [TEXT] [ENTER] [▼] [▼] [▼] [▼] [ENTER]
[ENTER] [ENTER]

LESSON 7.7
Technology Keystrokes
For use with Exercises 40 and 49 on pages 353 and 354

TI-34 II

40. `2nd` [MATH] `▶` `ENTER =` 14764 `÷` 5280 `2nd` [,] `)` `ENTER =`

49. `2nd` [MATH] `▶` `ENTER =` 6 `×` 4 `×` 2 `×` 2 `×` 8 `÷` 365

`2nd` [,] 0 `)` `ENTER =`

TI-73

40. `MATH` `▶` 2 14764 `÷` 5280 `,` 1 `)` `ENTER`

49. `MATH` `▶` 2 6 `×` 4 `×` 2 `×` 2 `×` 8 `÷` 365 `,` 0 `)` `ENTER`

LESSON 7.7

Practice A

For use with pages 348–355

Complete the statement.

1. $1 = \dfrac{1 \text{ mile}}{\underline{\quad?\quad} \text{ yard(s)}}$

2. $1 = \dfrac{2000 \text{ pounds}}{\underline{\quad?\quad} \text{ ton(s)}}$

3. $1 = \dfrac{1 \text{ gallon}}{\underline{\quad?\quad} \text{ quart(s)}}$

4. $1 = \dfrac{\underline{\quad?\quad} \text{ ounces}}{1 \text{ pound}}$

5. $1 = \dfrac{1 \text{ cup}}{\underline{\quad?\quad} \text{ fluid ounces}}$

6. $1 = \dfrac{3 \text{ feet}}{\underline{\quad?\quad} \text{ inches}}$

Complete the statement.

7. 3 T 400 lb = ___?___ lb

8. 4 mi 148 ft = 3 mi ___?___ ft

9. 5 qt 5 pt = 6 qt ___?___ pt

10. 180 in. = ___?___ yd ___?___ in., or ___?___ yd

11. 10 fl oz = 1 c ___?___ fl oz

12. 16 qt = ___?___ gal

Change the measurement to the specified unit.

13. 2 T to pounds

14. 7040 yd to miles

15. 48 fl oz to cups

16. 4 lb to ounces

17. 32 in. to feet

18. 41 qt to gallons

19. $\frac{3}{4}$ gal to quarts

20. 2500 lb to tons

21. $9\frac{1}{2}$ pt to quarts

Find the sum or difference.

22. $\begin{array}{r} 9 \text{ lb} \quad 7 \text{ oz} \\ + \ 3 \text{ lb} \quad 12 \text{ oz} \\ \hline \end{array}$

23. $\begin{array}{r} 1 \text{ gal} \quad 2 \text{ qt} \\ + \ 4 \text{ gal} \quad 3 \text{ qt} \\ \hline \end{array}$

24. $\begin{array}{r} 2 \text{ mi} \quad 90 \text{ ft} \\ + \ 1 \text{ mi} \quad 107 \text{ ft} \\ \hline \end{array}$

25. $\begin{array}{r} 5 \text{ T} \quad 187 \text{ lb} \\ - \ 1 \text{ T} \quad 213 \text{ lb} \\ \hline \end{array}$

26. $\begin{array}{r} 5 \text{ qt} \\ - \ 3 \text{ qt} \quad 1 \text{ pt} \\ \hline \end{array}$

27. $\begin{array}{r} 12 \text{ ft} \quad 3 \text{ in.} \\ - \ 10 \text{ ft} \quad 7 \text{ in} \\ \hline \end{array}$

28. A semi-truck can haul 40,000 pounds at one time. A trucking company wants to ship 22 tons of materials. Will they be able to ship all of the materials on one truck?

29. Your bedroom walls are 10 feet by 12 feet. You need to convert these measurements into yards in order to buy wallpaper. What are the measurements in yards?

30. A recipe calls for $2\frac{1}{2}$ quarts of strawberries. You only have strawberries that are in pint packages. How many of these packages will you need for this recipe?

Name _____ Date _____

Practice B

For use with pages 348–355

Match the given value with its equivalent value.

1. 1 mile   **A.** 1 ton

2. 2000 pounds   **B.** 12 inches

3. 4 quarts   **C.** 1760 yards

4. 1 foot   **D.** 2 pints

5. 1 pound   **E.** 16 ounces

6. 1 quart   **F.** 1 gallon

Complete the statement.

7. 1 T 850 lb = ___?___ lb

8. 2 qt 3 pt = 3 qt ___?___ pt

9. 7 mi 219 ft = 6 mi ___?___ ft

10. 252 in. = ___?___ yd ___?___ in., or ___?___ yd

11. 9 fl oz = 1 c ___?___ fl oz

12. 24 qt = ___?___ gal

Change the measurement to the specified unit.

13. 5 T to pounds

14. 3 mi to feet

15. 16 fl oz to cups

16. 48 oz to pounds

17. 19 in. to feet

18. 27 qt to gallons

19. $2\frac{1}{4}$ c to fl oz

20. $3\frac{3}{8}$ lb to ounces

21. $1\frac{7}{9}$ yd to inches

Find the sum or difference.

22.   6 lb   11 oz
      + 1 lb   15 oz

23.   5 gal   1 qt
      + 7 gal   3 qt

24.   3 mi   254 ft
      + 4 mi   706 ft

25.   4 T   408 lb
      − 3 T   855 lb

26.   4 qt
      − 2 qt   1 pt

27.   14 ft   6 in.
      − 8 ft   11 in.

Change the measurement to the specified unit.

28. 64 fl oz to quarts

29. 12 yd to inches

30. $3\frac{1}{2}$ gal to pints

31. You ran $26\frac{1}{5}$ miles in a marathon. What was the distance in yards? feet? inches?

Name _____ Date _____

7.7 Practice C

For use with pages 348–355

Which of the following are *not* equivalent?

1. 1 mile

   A. 1760 yards   **B.** 5280 feet   **C.** 31,680 inches

2. 4 quarts

   A. 1 gallon   **B.** 32 cups   **C.** 8 pints

3. 72 inches

   A. 1 mile   **B.** 6 feet   **C.** 2 yards

Complete the statement.

4. 3 T 712 lb = __?__ lb   **5.** 5 qt 1 pt = 4 qt __?__ pt

6. 6 mi 1702 yd = 5 mi __?__ yd   **7.** 240 in. = __?__ yd __?__ in.

8. 11 fl oz = 1 c __?__ fl oz   **9.** 48 qt = __?__ gal

Change the measurement to the specified unit.

10. 6 T to pounds   **11.** $1\frac{1}{2}$ mi to feet   **12.** 24 fl oz to cups

13. 80 oz to pounds   **14.** 233 in. to feet   **15.** 31 qt to gallons

16. $3\frac{3}{8}$ c to fl oz   **17.** $2\frac{3}{4}$ lb to ounces   **18.** $2\frac{5}{9}$ yd to inches

Find the sum or difference.

19.   3 lb   13 oz
       + 2 lb   12 oz

20.   3 gal   3 qt
       + 7 gal   3 qt

21.   1 mi   2247 ft
       + 6 mi   3745 ft

22.   5 T   1418 lb
       − 2 T   1853 lb

23.   4 qt
       − 3 qt   1 pt

24.   12 ft   3 in.
       − 6 ft   9 in.

Change the measurement to the specified unit.

25. 128 fl oz to quarts   **26.** 6 yd to inches   **27.** $2\frac{1}{4}$ gal to pints

28. You measure the length of your desk to be 24 inches. What is the length in feet? yards? miles?

Name _____ Date _____

Study Guide

For use with pages 348–355

GOAL Change customary units of measure.

VOCABULARY

You can multiply and divide using the following relationships to change from one customary unit to another.

Length	**Weight**	**Capacity**
1 ft = 12 in.	1 lb = 16 oz	1 c = 8 fl oz
1 yd = 3 ft = 36 in.	1 T = 2000 lb	1 pt = 2 c
1 mi = 1760 yd = 5280 ft		1 qt = 2 pt
		1 gal = 4 qt

You can change units by multiplying by a fraction that is equal to 1.

For example, 1 yd = 36 in., so $\frac{36 \text{ in.}}{1 \text{ yd}} = 1$.

EXAMPLE 1 **Changing Units Using Multiplication**

Change 4 lb 5 oz to ounces.

4 lb 5 oz = **4 lb** + 5 oz	Write the measure as a sum.
= **(4 × 16) oz** + 5 oz	Change the pounds to ounces.
= **64 oz** + 5 oz	Multiply.
= 69 oz	Add.

EXAMPLE 2 **Changing Units Using Division**

Change 41 inches to feet. Express the answer in two ways.

Solution

There are 12 inches in a foot, so divide 41 by 12.

$$\begin{array}{r} 3 \text{ R5} \\ 12\overline{)41} \\ 36 \\ \hline 5 \end{array}$$

You can interpret the remainder as 5 inches.

You can also interpret the remainder as $\frac{5}{12}$ feet, because the remaining division 5 ÷ 12 can be written as $\frac{5}{12}$.

Answer: There are 3 feet 5 inches in 41 inches, or $3\frac{5}{12}$ feet.

Exercises for Examples 1 and 2

Complete the statement.

1. 3 pt 1 c = __?__ c **2.** 1 mi 400 ft = __?__ ft **3.** 4 yd 7 in. = __?__ in.

4. 18 qt = __?__ gal **5.** 2500 lb = __?__ T **6.** 60 in. = __?__ yd

---

Name _____ Date _____

Study Guide

For use with pages 348–355

EXAMPLE 3 Multiplying by a Form of 1

Change $3\frac{1}{2}$ pt to quarts.

$$3\frac{1}{2} \text{ pt} = \frac{7 \text{ pt}}{2}$$ Write the measurement in fraction form.

$$= \frac{7 \text{ pt}}{2} \times \frac{1 \text{ qt}}{2 \text{ pt}}$$ Multiply by a form of 1. Use $\frac{1 \text{ qt}}{2 \text{ pt}}$.

$$= \frac{7}{4} \text{ qt, or } 1\frac{3}{4} \text{ qt}$$ Divide out "pt" so you are left with "qt."

EXAMPLE 4 Finding a Relationship

You make 1 quart of lemonade. How many fluid ounces is that?

Solution

Find the relationship between quarts and fluid ounces. Use the three relationships 1 qt = 2 pt, 1 pt = 2 c, and 1 c = 8 fl oz.

$$\frac{1 \text{ qt}}{2 \text{ pt}} \times \frac{1 \text{ pt}}{2 \text{ c}} \times \frac{1 \text{ c}}{8 \text{ fl oz}} = \frac{1 \text{ qt} \times 1 \text{ pt} \times 1 \text{ c}}{2 \text{ pt} \times 2 \text{ c} \times 8 \text{ fl oz}} = \frac{1 \text{ qt}}{32 \text{ fl oz}}$$

Answer: One quart is the same as 32 fluid ounces.

EXAMPLE 5 Adding and Subtracting Measurements

a. Add. Then rename the sum.

$$\begin{array}{r} 4 \text{ c} \quad 7 \text{ fl oz} \\ + 3 \text{ c} \quad 5 \text{ fl oz} \\ \hline 7 \text{ c} \quad 12 \text{ fl oz} \end{array}$$

Rename 7 c 12 fl oz as 8 c 4 fl oz.

Answer: The sum is 8 c 4 fl oz.

b. Rename one of the tons as pounds. Then subtract.

$$\begin{array}{r} 7 \text{ T} \quad 1200 \text{ lb} \\ - 2 \text{ T} \quad 1800 \text{ lb} \end{array} \longrightarrow \begin{array}{r} 6 \text{ T} \quad 3200 \text{ lb} \\ - 2 \text{ T} \quad 1800 \text{ lb} \\ \hline 4 \text{ T} \quad 1400 \text{ lb} \end{array}$$

Answer: The difference is 4 T 1400 lb.

Exercises for Examples 3–5

Change the measurement to the specified unit.

7. 30 in. to feet

8. 7 cups to pints

9. 18 fl oz to cups

Find the relationship.

10. How many inches are in $4\frac{1}{3}$ yards?

11. How many pints are in $3\frac{1}{4}$ gallons?

Find the sum or difference.

12.
$$\begin{array}{r} 7 \text{ pt} \quad 1 \text{ c} \\ + 6 \text{ pt} \quad 1 \text{ c} \\ \hline \end{array}$$

13.
$$\begin{array}{r} 6 \text{ yd} \quad 1 \text{ ft} \\ - 2 \text{ yd} \quad 2 \text{ ft} \\ \hline \end{array}$$

14.
$$\begin{array}{r} 5 \text{ qt} \quad 1 \text{ pt} \\ + 4 \text{ qt} \quad 1 \text{ pt} \\ \hline \end{array}$$

Real-World Problem Solving

For use with pages 348–355

Lawn Care

You are looking for a summer job to make money. You decide to try to make some money doing work for your neighbors. You create fliers and leave copies in your neighbors' doorways to let them know what kind of work you can do. Below is the information on the flier.

> Hi! I am your neighbor and I would like to do some lawn edging and bush trimming for you. My prices are:
>
> Lawn Edging: $2.00 per 5 yards
> Bush Trimming: $1.00 per yard of bushes
>
> Please call 555-1234 for an estimate.

In Exercises 1–5, use the following information.

You receive five phone calls from neighbors asking for estimates.
You use a tape measure in feet to find measurements at each neighbor's house. Before you calculate the estimates, you will need to convert the measurements into yards.

Convert each length to yards.

1. Mr. Balog: 325 feet of edging; 14 feet of bushes

2. Mrs. Emerson: 422 feet of edging; 9 feet of bushes

3. Mr. Rios: 388 feet of edging; 16 feet of bushes

4. Mr. Chen: 400 feet of edging; 20 feet of bushes

5. Ms. Widowson: 376 feet of edging; 11 feet of bushes

Lesson 7.7

LESSON 7.7

Challenge Practice

For use with pages 348–355

1. In the United States, the average person uses about 73 gallons of water per day. Change this measurement to cups per hour. Round to the nearest whole number.

2. At 1:15 P.M., a 40-gallon hot water tank begins to leak water at a rate of 2 tablespoons per second. If no more water is added to the tank, at what time will the tank be empty? (*Hint:* 1 tablespoon $\approx \frac{1}{2}$ fluid ounce) Round to the nearest minute.

3. If a camel is very thirsty, it can drink 30 gallons of water in 10 minutes. How many cups of water is that per second? Round to the nearest whole number.

4. A 2 liter bottle of soda costs $1.09, and a 20-fluid ounce bottle costs $.79. Find the cost per ounce for each size of bottle (1 L is about 1.06 qt). Round to the nearest cent. Which bottle of soda is the better buy?

5. The average person loses 2 pounds per week on a special diet. How many ounces per day is that? Round to the nearest whole number.

6. A car is traveling 65 miles per hour on an interstate highway. What is the car's speed in feet per second? Round to the nearest second.

Name _____ Date _____

Chapter Review Games and Activities

For use after Chapter 7

Skill Race

Players: 2–4

Getting Started: Without looking at the problems, each player chooses a column.

Object: The first player to correctly finish all of the problems in his/her column wins.

A	B	C	D
$8 \times \frac{1}{4}$	$6 \times \frac{1}{3}$	$10 \times \frac{1}{5}$	$21 \times \frac{1}{3}$
$10 \times \frac{5}{6}$	$4 \times \frac{5}{8}$	$12 \times \frac{3}{8}$	$5 \times \frac{7}{10}$
$\frac{1}{6} \times \frac{5}{7}$	$\frac{2}{5} \times \frac{2}{7}$	$\frac{9}{10} \times \frac{1}{2}$	$\frac{2}{3} \times \frac{5}{9}$
$\frac{9}{10} \times \frac{5}{6}$	$\frac{3}{5} \times \frac{10}{21}$	$\frac{6}{7} \times \frac{14}{15}$	$\frac{2}{3} \times \frac{9}{14}$
$\frac{2}{5} \times \frac{3}{4} \times \frac{5}{12}$	$\frac{1}{4} \times \frac{6}{7} \times \frac{7}{24}$	$\frac{3}{8} \times \frac{2}{9} \times \frac{4}{9}$	$\frac{5}{6} \times \frac{9}{20} \times \frac{8}{15}$
$2\frac{1}{4} \times 3$	$5\frac{2}{3} \times 2$	$4\frac{2}{5} \times 3$	$3\frac{1}{3} \times 4$
$6\frac{1}{7} \times \frac{3}{5}$	$3\frac{3}{5} \times \frac{2}{3}$	$1\frac{4}{9} \times \frac{1}{4}$	$2\frac{1}{3} \times \frac{1}{2}$
$1\frac{7}{8} \times 2\frac{2}{3}$	$5\frac{1}{2} \times 2\frac{1}{2}$	$3\frac{3}{4} \times 1\frac{1}{5}$	$3\frac{2}{7} \times 4\frac{1}{5}$
$\frac{2}{3} \div \frac{1}{4}$	$\frac{3}{4} \div \frac{2}{3}$	$\frac{3}{5} \div \frac{1}{4}$	$\frac{2}{7} \div \frac{5}{6}$
$\frac{4}{7} \div 3$	$\frac{2}{5} \div 6$	$\frac{1}{3} \div 2$	$\frac{5}{9} \div 4$
$2\frac{2}{5} \div \frac{4}{7}$	$5\frac{1}{3} \div \frac{4}{9}$	$3\frac{2}{7} \div \frac{5}{12}$	$6\frac{2}{3} \div \frac{4}{5}$
$6\frac{1}{5} \div 8$	$4\frac{7}{8} \div 5$	$2\frac{13}{15} \div 3$	$4\frac{2}{5} \div 2$
$4\frac{3}{8} \div 2\frac{1}{4}$	$3\frac{11}{12} \div 1\frac{3}{8}$	$5\frac{2}{9} \div 2\frac{1}{2}$	$3\frac{7}{15} \div 4\frac{1}{10}$

Review and Projects

CHAPTER 7

Real-Life Project: Musical Notes

For use after Chapter 7

Objective In this project, you will learn how musical notes are measured.

Materials pencil, paper

Investigation Musical notes are measured according to their frequency. Frequency is how high or low a note sounds. The unit of measurement for frequency is the hertz (Hz). A group of 8 consecutive notes and their frequencies are shown in the table below. These 8 notes make up the C major scale. The frequency of each note in the scale is found by multiplying the previous note's frequency by an appropriate fraction.

C Major Scale								
Note	C	D	E	F	G	A	B	C
Frequency	264 Hz	297 Hz	330 Hz	352 Hz	396 Hz	440 Hz	495 Hz	528 Hz

$$\times \frac{9}{8} \quad \times \frac{10}{9} \quad \times \frac{16}{15} \quad \times \frac{9}{8} \quad \times \frac{10}{9} \quad \times \frac{9}{8} \quad \times \frac{16}{15}$$

When you start with any note and create a scale of 8 consecutive notes, the frequencies are always found in the same way. The 2nd frequency is the 1st frequency multiplied by $\frac{9}{8}$, the 3rd frequency is the 2nd frequency multiplied by $\frac{10}{9}$, and so on.

1. Continue the C major scale by completing the table below.

Continuation of C Major Scale							
Note	C	D	E	F	G	A	B	C
Frequency	528 Hz	___ Hz	___ Hz	___ Hz	___ Hz	___ Hz	___ Hz	___ Hz

2. Complete the table to find the note frequencies for the G major scale.

G Major Scale							
Note	G	A	B	C	D	E	F	G
Frequency	396 Hz	___ Hz	___ Hz	___ Hz	___ Hz	___ Hz	___ Hz	___ Hz

3. Compare each note in the G major scale to the note with the same name in the C major scales, starting at G with 396 hertz. For which notes are the frequencies different? If the difference is greater than 10 hertz, then the note is called a sharp if its frequency is greater than the corresponding frequency in C major, or the note is called a flat if its frequency is less than the corresponding frequency in C major. Which notes in the G major scale are sharps or flats?

4. Create your own scale of 8 consecutive notes by choosing a note from the C major scale. Notice that the notes are in alphabetical order from A to G. G is then always followed by A, B, C, and so on. Then find the frequencies of the notes.

5. Find any flats or sharps in your scale.

Review and Projects

Name _____ Date _____

Teacher's Notes for Musical Notes

For use after Chapter 7

Project Goals • Multiply fractions and whole numbers.

• Subtract decimals.

Managing the Project

Guiding Students' Work Make sure that the students understand that the note names repeatedly cycle through A, B, C, D, E, F, and G. They should also understand that when they are comparing notes from the G major scale (or the scale they choose) to the notes from the C major scale that these are the same notes, with the exception of the sharps and flats. You can illustrate this point with the following diagram.

C Major Scale	G Major Scale
C	G
D	A
E	B
F	C
G	D
A	E
B	F
C	G

Rubric for Project

The following rubric can be used to assess student work.

4 The student correctly finds the frequencies for the continuation of the C major scale and the G major scale. The student chooses his or her own scale and correctly identifies the notes and their frequencies. The sharps or flats for the G major scale and the student's chosen scale are correctly identified.

3 The student finds the frequencies for the continuation of the C major scale and the G major scale, but makes minor errors. The student chooses his or her own scale and correctly identifies the notes with minor errors in the frequencies. The sharps or flats for the G major scale and the student's chosen scale are identified according to his or her calculations for all the scales.

2 The student finds the frequencies for the continuation of the C major scale and the G major scale, but makes some errors. The student chooses his or her own scale and correctly identifies the notes, but makes some errors when finding the frequencies. Most of the sharps or flats for the G major scale and the student's chosen scale are identified according to his or her calculations for all the scales.

1 The student makes many errors when finding all the frequencies and some of the frequencies are missing. The student does not correctly identify the sharps or flats for either scale.

Review and Projects

Cooperative Project: Card Game

For use after Chapter 7

Objective   In this project, you will create and play a card game that helps you practice fraction operations.

Materials   paper, pencil, index cards

Investigation   Creating the Game

A deck of cards will be created from 75 index cards. Create your deck as follows.

Write each fraction on 2 separate cards:

$$\frac{1}{2}, \frac{1}{3}, \frac{2}{3}, \frac{1}{4}, \frac{3}{4}, \frac{1}{5}, \frac{2}{5}, \frac{3}{5}, \frac{4}{5}, \frac{1}{6}, \frac{5}{6}, \frac{1}{7}, \frac{2}{7}, \frac{3}{7}, \frac{4}{7}, \frac{5}{7}, \frac{6}{7}, \frac{1}{8}, \frac{3}{8}, \frac{5}{8}, \frac{7}{8}, \frac{1}{9}, \frac{2}{9}, \frac{4}{9}, \frac{5}{9}, \frac{7}{9}, \frac{8}{9}$$

Write each number on a single card:

$$\frac{3}{2}, \frac{4}{3}, \frac{8}{3}, \frac{5}{4}, \frac{7}{4}, \frac{6}{5}, \frac{8}{5}, \frac{7}{6}, \frac{11}{6}, \frac{8}{7}, \frac{9}{7}, \frac{10}{9}, \frac{11}{9}, 2, 3, 4, 5, 6, 7, 8, 9$$

Playing the Game

First, choose a person to deal the cards and another person to keep score. After the deck is shuffled, the dealer should give 10 cards to each player.

To play the game, a card is turned face up from the deck. The goal is for each player to choose an operation (addition, subtraction, multiplication, or division) and one of the cards in the player's hand so that the sum, difference, product, or quotient of the card from the deck and the card from the player's hand is as close to 1 as possible.

Once all players have had enough time to make their choice, each player lays down his/her card and states the operation his/her is using. The score keeper records the value of the card, the operation used, and the answer found using that operation. The group now needs to determine which player's choice is the closest to 1. The player closest to 1 gets a point and all of the used cards get shuffled back into the deck. If two or more players get the same value for the closest value to 1, then no point will be awarded.

Continue playing the game with the dealer turning over another card from the deck and each player choosing another card from his/her hand and an operation so that the sum, difference, product, or quotient is as close to 1 as possible. The game ends when all players are out of cards. The player with the most points wins.

Name _____ Date _____

Teacher's Notes for
Card Game Project

For use after Chapter 7

Project Goals • Add, subtract, multiply, and divide fractions and/or whole numbers.

• Order fractions.

Managing the Project *Classroom Management*   This project will work well for groups of 3 to 5 people. You can make the game more challenging for students by having them use two or three of their cards in combination with the card from the deck. If you choose to do this, the students should begin the game with a greater number of cards.

Rubric for Project **The following rubric can be used to assess student work.**

4 The students follow the directions. The record of the game is neatly kept. The sums, differences, products, and quotients are correct and the students identify which is closest to 1.

3 The students follow the directions. The record of the game is neatly kept. The sums, differences, products, and quotients are mostly correct and the students identify which is closest to 1.

2 The students have a little trouble following the directions. The record of the game is a little sloppy. The students make more than a few errors when calculating the sums, differences, products, and quotients and when identifying which is closest to 1.

1 The students do not follow the directions. The record of the game is sloppy. The students make many errors when calculating the sums, differences, products, and quotients and when identifying which is closest to 1.

Review and Projects

Name _____ Date _____

Independent Extra Credit Project: Recipes

For use after Chapter 7

Objective   Determine quantities of ingredients you need when making more than one batch of a recipe.

Materials   paper, pencil

Investigation   In recipes, wet and dry ingredients are measured using capacity measures like teaspoons, tablespoons, and cups. Wet ingredients are sold using capacity measures like pints and gallons, but dry ingredients are sold using weight measures like ounces and pounds. As a result, finding out how many cups are in a 5-pound bag of flour can be challenging. The table below shows the relationships between weight and capacity measures for some commonly used dry ingredients.

Ingredient	Weight	Capacity		Ingredient	Weight	Capacity
Flour	1 pound	$3\frac{1}{2}$ cups		Salt	1 pound	$31\frac{1}{3}$ tablespoons
Sugar	1 pound	$2\frac{1}{4}$ cups		Baking Powder	1 ounce	6 teaspoons
Butter	1 pound	32 tablespoons		Baking Soda	1 ounce	6 teaspoons

1. Complete the table below for the standard selling quantities of some dry ingredients.

Ingredient	Quantity	Capacity		Ingredient	Quantity	Capacity
Flour	5-lb bag	___ cups		Butter	$\frac{1}{2}$-lb tub	___ tablespoons
Sugar	5-lb bag	___ cups		Baking Powder	7-oz can	___ teaspoons
Salt	3-lb box	___ tablespoons		Baking Soda	16-oz box	___ teaspoons

2. Find a recipe for an item that you can easily serve to your class like bread or muffins. How many people does one batch of your recipe serve? How many batches do you need in order for every person in your class to have at least one serving? Note: You should only make a whole number of batches.

3. According to your recipe, how much of each ingredient will you need for all the batches? Give the amount of each ingredient in the unit used in the recipe. For instance, if the recipe calls for 1 cup of flour and you need to make 5 batches, you need $1 \times 5 = 5$ cups of flour.

4. Determine the number of bags, containers, boxes, etc., you will need for each dry ingredient in your recipe that is mentioned in the table above.

5. Find the selling quantities for the wet ingredients (milk, vanilla, etc.) in your recipe. Then determine the number of these that you need for your recipe. Common conversions that may be useful for this step:

   6 teaspoons = 2 tablespoons = 1 fluid ounce.

Name _____ Date _____

Teacher's Notes for Recipes Project

For use after Chapter 7

Project Goals
- Change customary units of measure.
- Multiply and divide mixed numbers and whole numbers.

Managing the Project

Guiding Students' Work Inform your students that unless otherwise instructed, they are to use the conversions in Lesson 7.7 for changing units. For example, wet ingredients like milk and vanilla should use the capacity conversions found on page 350 of the text. You may want to provide the students with common selling quantities of wet ingredients. For instance, milk is sold by the quart and vanilla is sold by the fluid ounce.

Rubric for Project

The following rubric can be used to assess student work.

4 The student correctly makes the conversions for the dry ingredients in the table. The student finds a recipe. The number of batches and the amount of each ingredient needed are correctly determined. The student correctly finds the number of bags, boxes, etc., needed for each ingredient.

3 The student makes the conversions for the dry ingredients in the table, but makes a couple of errors. The student finds a recipe. The number of batches is correctly determined. The student makes a few errors when finding the amount of each ingredient needed. The student correctly finds the number of bags, boxes, etc., needed for each ingredient according to the amounts of ingredients the student has calculated.

2 The student makes many errors when completing the table of conversions. The student finds a recipe. The number of batches is correctly determined. The student makes errors when finding the amount of each ingredient needed. The student correctly finds the number of bags, boxes, etc., for most of the ingredients.

1 The student makes many errors and omissions in the table of conversions. The student may not provide a valid recipe, and does not correctly find the number of batches needed. The student makes many errors when finding the amount of each ingredient needed. The student makes many errors finding the number of bags, boxes, etc., for the ingredients.

Name _____ Date _____

Cumulative Practice

For use after Chapter 7

Evaluate the expression when $x = 2$ and $y = 7$. (Lessons 1.3–1.5)

1. $19 - y + x^3$ **2.** $12 \div x + y$ **3.** $x^4 - 2y$

Find the length of the segment to the nearest tenth of a centimeter. (Lesson 3.2)

4.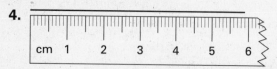

5.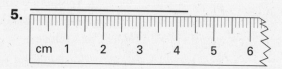

The circle graph shows the number of hours a student spends on various activities during a typical 24-hour school day. (Lessons 2.7, 6.4, 6.5)

6. How many hours are spent on "other" activities?

7. Predict how many hours the student will study during a 5-day school week.

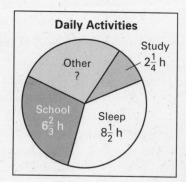

Daily Activities

Find the sum, difference, product, or quotient.
(Lessons 4.3–4.6, 6.2–6.5)

8. $74 - 39$ **9.** 15×23 **10.** $7.6 - 3.96$ **11.** 2.17×5

12. 4.91×0.6 **13.** $7.42 \div 9$ **14.** 5.02×0.01 **15.** $25.5 \div 0.12$

16. $\dfrac{7}{8} - \dfrac{2}{8}$ **17.** $\dfrac{5}{6} + \dfrac{1}{6}$ **18.** $\dfrac{1}{8} + \dfrac{3}{4}$ **19.** $\dfrac{23}{24} - \dfrac{5}{6}$

20. $3\dfrac{2}{7} + 5\dfrac{3}{7}$ **21.** $3\dfrac{3}{4} - 1\dfrac{3}{8}$ **22.** $5\dfrac{1}{3} - 2\dfrac{2}{3}$ **23.** $4 - \dfrac{3}{10}$

Order the numbers from least to greatest. (Lessons 3.3, 5.5)

24. $1.21, 1.12, 1.024$ **25.** $0.7, 0.68, 0.71$

26. $\dfrac{11}{15}, \dfrac{13}{15}, \dfrac{8}{15}$ **27.** $\dfrac{1}{7}, \dfrac{1}{6}, \dfrac{1}{9}$

Use the distributive property to evaluate the expression.
(Lesson 4.2)

28. $3(10 + 9)$ **29.** $8(60 + 3)$ **30.** $5(37)$ **31.** $4(42)$

Review and Projects

Name _____ Date _____

Cumulative Practice

For use after Chapter 7

Complete the statement. (Lessons 3.2, 4.8)

32. 3 and 2 hundredths meters = ___?___ meters

33. 10 and 4 tenths meters = ___?___ meters

34. 76 mm = ___?___ cm

35. 0.2 kg = ___?___ g

36. 525 mL = ___?___ L

Test the number for divisibility by 2, 3, 5, 6, 9, and 10. (Lesson 5.1)

37. 96   **38.** 105   **39.** 315   **40.** 430

Find the GCF and LCM of the numbers. (Lessons 5.2, 5.4)

41. 12, 24   **42.** 24, 30   **43.** 14, 35   **44.** 36, 42

Complete the statement. (Lessons 5.3, 5.6)

45. $\frac{6}{7} = \frac{?}{42}$ **46.** $\frac{28}{52} = \frac{7}{?}$ **47.** $\frac{11}{3} = 3\frac{?}{3}$ **48.** $4\frac{2}{9} = \frac{?}{9}$

Add or subtract the measures of time. (Lesson 6.6)

49.   3 h 45 min
     +   25 min

50.   5 h 32 min
     − 2 h 12 min

51.   4 h 30 min
     − 1 h 50 min

Find the product or quotient. (Lessons 7.1–7.5)

52. $2 \times \frac{2}{3}$ **53.** $\frac{5}{16} \times 3$

54. $\frac{2}{3} \times \frac{4}{7}$ **55.** $\frac{1}{2} \times \frac{3}{8}$

56. $2\frac{1}{4} \times \frac{7}{8}$ **57.** $2\frac{1}{2} \times 2\frac{1}{3}$

58. $\frac{7}{8} \div \frac{3}{4}$ **59.** $\frac{14}{5} \div \frac{1}{15}$

60. $6 \div \frac{2}{3}$ **61.** $7\frac{1}{5} \div 4$

62. $4\frac{7}{8} \div \frac{1}{4}$ **63.** $5\frac{2}{3} \div \frac{4}{9}$

Review and Projects

Answers

Lesson 7.1

Practice A

1. $5 \times \frac{3}{4}$ **2.** $\frac{6}{7}$ **3.** $\frac{5}{8}$ **4.** 3 **5.** 2 **6.** $9\frac{3}{5}$

7. 16 **8.** $6\frac{6}{7}$ **9.** $2\frac{1}{2}$ **10.** $8\frac{8}{9}$ **11.** 12; 2

12. 6; 4 **13.** 10; 8 **14.** 16; 10 **15.** 12; 3

16. 20; 14 **17.** 45 minutes **18.** 14 inches

19. $4 **20.** 25 chocolate cupcakes

21. 3 cinnamon raisin bagels

Practice B

1. $6 \times \frac{2}{3}$ **2.** $3\frac{1}{3}$ **3.** 5 **4.** $2\frac{2}{5}$ **5.** $1\frac{1}{3}$ **6.** $2\frac{6}{13}$

7. $5\frac{1}{4}$ **8.** $13\frac{1}{8}$ **9.** 6 **10.** $7\frac{3}{7}$ **11.** 6; 4

12. 18; 8 **13.** 12; 10 **14.** 24; 4 **15.** 30; 24

16. 18; 14 **17.** $40 **18.** win 20 games; lose 12 games **19.** 24 children; 7 senior citizens

20. 30 goldfish

Practice C

1. $3\frac{1}{5}$ **2.** $1\frac{2}{7}$ **3.** $3\frac{3}{4}$ **4.** $6\frac{2}{9}$ **5.** $1\frac{7}{11}$ **6.** $7\frac{1}{2}$

7. $7\frac{1}{12}$ **8.** $3\frac{1}{2}$ **9.** $26\frac{2}{5}$ **10.** 10; 4 **11.** 12; 9

12. 18; 15 **13.** 21; 9 **14.** 36; 33 **15.** 18; 14

16. 78 **17.** 60 **18.** 126 **19.** $\frac{1}{3}$: less than 45; 15; $\frac{2}{3}$: less than 45; 30; $\frac{4}{5}$: less than 45; 36; $\frac{7}{5}$: greater than 45; 63; $\frac{5}{9}$: less than 45; 25; $\frac{10}{9}$: greater than 45; 50; $\frac{11}{15}$: less than 45; 33

20. 10 maple trees **21.** 100 dogwood trees

22. 60 elm and maple trees **23.** 60

24. You have 31 cards and your friend has 29 cards.

Study Guide

1. $\frac{10}{3}$ or $3\frac{1}{3}$ **2.** $\frac{3}{2}$ or $1\frac{1}{2}$ **3.** $\frac{12}{5}$ or $2\frac{2}{5}$

4. $\frac{7}{4}$ or $1\frac{3}{4}$ **5.** $\frac{5}{2}$ or $2\frac{1}{2}$ **6.** 6 **7.** $\frac{8}{3}$ or $2\frac{2}{3}$

8. $\frac{9}{2}$ or $4\frac{1}{2}$ **9.** $\frac{7}{6}$ or $1\frac{1}{6}$ **10.** $\frac{3}{2}$ or $1\frac{1}{2}$

11. $\frac{5}{2}$ or $2\frac{1}{2}$ **12.** $\frac{9}{4}$ or $2\frac{1}{4}$

13. 5 **14.** 3

15. 8

16. 4 **17.** 15 **18.** 6 **19.** 3 **20.** 4 **21.** 2

22. 10 **23.** 4 **24.** 9

Challenge Practice

1. $149\frac{1}{11}$ psi **2.** $5678\frac{7}{11}$ psi **3.** $83\frac{2}{11}$ psi

4. $194\frac{6}{11}$ psi **5.** $117\frac{3}{11}$ psi

Lesson 7.2

Practice A

1. **2.** $\frac{1}{15}$ **3.** $\frac{3}{56}$ **4.** $\frac{2}{9}$ **5.** $\frac{7}{20}$

6. $\frac{8}{21}$ **7.** $\frac{1}{9}$ **8.** $\frac{5}{44}$ **9.** $\frac{9}{32}$ **10.** $\frac{7}{18}$ **11.** $\frac{5}{48}$

12. $\frac{1}{8}$ **13.** $\frac{3}{22}$ **14.** $\frac{7}{108}$ **15.** $\frac{2}{63}$ **16.** $\frac{32}{105}$

17. $\frac{8}{57}$ **18.** $\frac{1}{4}$ mile **19.** $\frac{1}{8}$ cup of oil

20. $\frac{3}{20}$ yard of material

Practice B

1. $\frac{1}{4} \times \frac{3}{8}$ **2.** $\frac{4}{15}$ **3.** $\frac{3}{28}$ **4.** $\frac{3}{10}$ **5.** $\frac{7}{16}$ **6.** $\frac{4}{11}$

7. $\frac{3}{5}$ **8.** $\frac{55}{72}$ **9.** $\frac{5}{48}$ **10.** $\frac{80}{231}$ **11.** $\frac{1}{2}$ **12.** $\frac{14}{27}$

13. $\frac{11}{24}$ **14.** < **15.** > **16.** < **17.** = **18.** <

19. < **20.** $\frac{5}{18}$ of an hour **21.** $\frac{5}{12}$ of an hour

22. $\frac{5}{36}$ of an hour

Practice C

1. $\frac{1}{4}$ **2.** $\frac{11}{16}$ **3.** $\frac{40}{63}$ **4.** $\frac{8}{45}$ **5.** $\frac{12}{55}$ **6.** $\frac{35}{72}$

7. $\frac{1}{4}$ **8.** $\frac{35}{216}$ **9.** $\frac{2}{21}$ **10.** $\frac{15}{56}$ **11.** $\frac{20}{77}$ **12.** $\frac{5}{12}$

13. < **14.** < **15.** = **16.** > **17.** < **18.** >

Lesson 7.2 *continued*

19. $\frac{2}{5}$ **20.** $\frac{31}{36}$ **21.** $\frac{8}{147}$ **22.** $\frac{6}{475}$ **23.** $\frac{25}{234}$

24. $\frac{56}{275}$ **25.** $\frac{5}{6} \times \frac{1}{30}, \frac{5}{6} \times \frac{3}{16}, \frac{5}{6} \times \frac{1}{2}, \frac{5}{6} \times \frac{8}{9}, \frac{5}{6} \times \frac{21}{20}$

The fractions are increasing in size; therefore, the product will also increase in size.

26. 150 families

Study Guide

1.  $\frac{1}{12}$ **2.** $\frac{2}{15}$

3. $\frac{5}{12}$

4. $\frac{3}{32}$ **5.** $\frac{1}{4}$ **6.** $\frac{8}{15}$ **7.** $\frac{5}{28}$ **8.** $\frac{4}{27}$ **9.** $\frac{5}{12}$

10. $\frac{1}{20}$ **11.** $\frac{5}{36}$ **12.** $\frac{3}{28}$ **13.** $\frac{3}{14}$ **14.** 1 **15.** $\frac{1}{6}$

Challenge Practice

1. $\frac{1}{4} \times \frac{2}{3} = \frac{2}{12} = \frac{1}{6}$ **2.** $\frac{5}{6} \times \frac{1}{6} = \frac{5}{36}$

3. $\frac{8}{9} \times \frac{1}{2} = \frac{8}{18} = \frac{4}{9}$ **4.** $\frac{3}{4} \times \frac{5}{6} = \frac{15}{24} = \frac{5}{8}$

5. $\frac{1}{5}$ **6.** $\frac{1}{63}$ **7.** $\frac{5}{28}$ **8.** $\frac{1}{21}$

9. $\frac{13}{4} \cdot \frac{13}{9} = \frac{169}{36} = \frac{13}{4} + \frac{13}{9}$; No. *Sample Answer:*
$\frac{11}{6} + \frac{11}{9} = \frac{55}{18}$ and $\frac{11}{6} \times \frac{11}{9} = \frac{121}{54}$.

Lesson 7.3

Practice A

1. $\frac{11}{24}$ **2.** $\frac{11}{30}$ **3.** 14 **4.** $4\frac{1}{5}$ **5.** $26\frac{13}{14}$ **6.** $3\frac{31}{96}$

7. $47\frac{3}{10}$ **8.** $10\frac{2}{7}$ **9.** $1\frac{7}{8}$ **10.** $10\frac{6}{7}$ **11.** $5\frac{3}{5}$

12. $17\frac{1}{4}$ **13.** yes, the fractions reduce to $\frac{2}{7} \times \frac{1}{1}$.

14. no **15.** yes, the fractions reduce to $\frac{1}{3} \times \frac{1}{2}$.

16. 15 **17.** 49 **18.** 6 **19.** $6\frac{34}{45}$ square yards

20. $7\frac{19}{32}$ square meters **21.** $29\frac{1}{2}$ minutes

22. $20\frac{7}{10}$ dollars **23.** $27\frac{13}{16}$ square feet

Practice B

1. $1\frac{7}{12}$ **2.** $\frac{9}{10}$ **3.** $7\frac{1}{3}$ **4.** $24\frac{4}{5}$ **5.** $18\frac{38}{99}$

6. $1\frac{17}{28}$ **7.** $26\frac{26}{27}$ **8.** 4 **9.** $7\frac{11}{16}$ **10.** 15

11. $30\frac{147}{187}$ **12.** $23\frac{167}{315}$ **13.** 20 **14.** 4 **15.** 16

16. $17\frac{3}{11}$ square centimeters **17.** $2\frac{4}{13}$ square feet

18. $3\frac{1}{2}$ miles **19.** $4\frac{1}{10}$ miles

20. $4\frac{7}{10}$ miles; $16\frac{9}{20}$ miles

Practice C

1. 8 **2.** $2\frac{8}{35}$ **3.** $4\frac{7}{8}$ **4.** $7\frac{3}{5}$ **5.** $16\frac{7}{13}$ **6.** $4\frac{67}{77}$

7. $18\frac{8}{9}$ **8.** $28\frac{3}{5}$ **9.** $54\frac{11}{16}$ **10.** $22\frac{2}{9}$

11. $140\frac{6}{7}$ **12.** $80\frac{15}{32}$ **13.** 22 **14.** 42 **15.** 16

16. $10\frac{2}{9}$ square meters **17.** $25\frac{43}{77}$ square inches

18. $39\frac{1}{3}$ **19.** He will not reach his goal.

20. $187\frac{59}{64}$ dollars **21.** $356\frac{2}{7}$ miles; She will need to fill her gas tank twice.

Study Guide

1. $\frac{9}{10}$ **2.** $\frac{20}{21}$ **3.** $1\frac{13}{15}$ **4.** $\frac{3}{8}$ **5.** $5\frac{1}{4}$ **6.** $13\frac{1}{2}$

7. 15 **8.** 4 **9.** 3 **10.** 2 **11.** 14 **12.** $\frac{40}{3}$

13. $\frac{10}{3}$ or $3\frac{1}{3}$ in.^{2} **14.** $\frac{39}{8}$ or $4\frac{7}{8}$ yd^2

15. $\frac{49}{12}$ or $4\frac{1}{12}$ m^2

Challenge Practice

1. $2\frac{1}{3}$ h **2.** 3:00 P.M. **3.** $6\frac{5}{12}$ h **4.** 11:20 A.M.

5. $1\frac{58}{75}$ h **6.** about 4:44 P.M. **7.** $2\frac{8}{15}$ h

8. $2\frac{4}{5}$ h

Lesson 7.4

Practice A

1. yes **2.** no **3.** yes **4.** $\frac{3}{2}$ **5.** 9 **6.** $\frac{1}{5}$

7. $\frac{8}{7}$ **8.** $\frac{1}{4}$ **9.** $\frac{10}{3}$ **10.** $\frac{1}{4} \times \frac{8}{3}; \frac{2}{3}$

11. $\frac{1}{6} \times \frac{9}{2}; \frac{3}{4}$ **12.** $8 \times \frac{13}{12}; 8\frac{2}{3}$ **13.** $\frac{1}{5}$ **14.** $1\frac{1}{2}$

15. $1\frac{13}{15}$ **16.** $\frac{2}{11}$ **17.** $1\frac{1}{2}$ **18.** $1\frac{1}{2}$ **19.** 3

20. $\frac{2}{15}$ **21.** $16\frac{4}{5}$ **22.** $8 \div \frac{2}{3}$ **23.** 12

24. 12 = number of days **25.** 8 **26.** $4\frac{1}{2}$

Practice B

1. 3 **2.** $\frac{5}{4}$ **3.** $\frac{1}{7}$ **4.** $\frac{11}{6}$ **5.** $\frac{1}{18}$ **6.** $\frac{13}{2}$ **7.** $\frac{4}{3}$

8. $\frac{1}{5}$ **9.** 1 **10.** 3; 24 **11.** 10; 4; 40 **12.** $\frac{2}{5}$

13. $\frac{3}{4}$ **14.** 18 **15.** $\frac{6}{7}$ **16.** $\frac{3}{16}$ **17.** $\frac{7}{9}$

Lesson 7.4 *continued*

18. $1\frac{2}{25}$ **19.** $\frac{13}{85}$ **20.** 55 **21.** $\frac{2}{7}$ **22.** $\frac{7}{40}$

23. $3\frac{1}{2}$ **24.** $22\frac{6}{7}$ **25.** $\frac{7}{10}$ **26.** $\frac{2}{35}$ **27.** $1\frac{2}{19}$

28. 60 words per minute **29.** 48 pieces; They will not have enough pie.

Practice C

1. 4 **2.** $\frac{7}{4}$ **3.** $\frac{1}{12}$ **4.** $\frac{14}{5}$ **5.** $\frac{1}{3}$ **6.** $\frac{13}{9}$ **7.** $\frac{9}{7}$

8. $\frac{1}{3}$ **9.** 1 **10.** 4; 24 **11.** $\frac{12}{17}; \frac{5}{4}; \frac{15}{17}$ **12.** $\frac{3}{11}$

13. $\frac{22}{45}$ **14.** $2\frac{8}{9}$ **15.** 18 **16.** $1\frac{1}{2}$ **17.** $\frac{23}{50}$

18. $1\frac{1}{39}$ **19.** $\frac{4}{15}$ **20.** 30 **21.** $1\frac{1}{25}$ **22.** $\frac{55}{108}$

23. $\frac{23}{108}$ **24.** $2\frac{7}{10}$ **25.** $\frac{1}{18}$ **26.** $\frac{10}{27}$ **27.** 30

28. $\frac{5}{54}$ **29.** $\frac{27}{40}$ **30.** = **31.** > **32.** <

33. 72 beats per minute

Study Guide

1. $\frac{6}{5}$ **2.** $\frac{5}{8}$ **3.** $\frac{1}{11}$ **4.** $\frac{2}{3}$ **5.** $3\frac{3}{7}$ **6.** $\frac{4}{5}$

7. 4 **8.** $\frac{3}{4}$ **9.** $\frac{3}{20}$ **10.** $\frac{5}{24}$ **11.** 14

Challenge Practice

1. $\frac{3}{4}$ mm **2.** $\frac{7}{8}$ in. **3.** $4 \div \frac{1}{4} = 16$

4. $2 \div \frac{1}{8} = 16$ **5.** $\frac{4}{15}$ **6.** $\frac{9}{10}$ **7.** $\frac{2}{3}$ **8.** $\frac{7}{9}$

Lesson 7.5

Technology Keystrokes

1. $2\frac{4}{21}$ **2.** $1\frac{13}{44}$ **3.** $3\frac{6}{7}$ **4.** $2\frac{1}{2}$ **5.** $2\frac{87}{170}$

6. $7\frac{1}{15}$ **7.** $3\frac{3}{8}$ **8.** $10\frac{2}{3}$ **9.** $2\frac{181}{333}$ **10.** $8\frac{125}{272}$

11. $33\frac{68}{189}$ **12.** $83\frac{61}{63}$ **13.** $20\frac{4}{11}$ miles per gallon

14. $27\frac{1}{2}$ gallons **15.** $11\frac{3}{7}$ servings **16.** 28 cups

Activity Master

1 and 2.

	Write as improper fractions	Quotient (Number of tally marks)
$3\frac{3}{4} \div 1\frac{1}{4}$	$\frac{15}{4} \div \frac{5}{4}$	3
$6 \div 1\frac{1}{2}$	$\frac{12}{2} \div \frac{3}{2}$	4
$6\frac{1}{4} \div 1\frac{1}{4}$	$\frac{25}{4} \div \frac{5}{4}$	5
$5\frac{1}{3} \div 2\frac{2}{3}$	$\frac{16}{3} \div \frac{8}{3}$	2

3. *Sample Answer:* Find the quotient of the numerators.

Practice A

1. C **2.** A **3.** D **4.** E **5.** B

6. They are not reciprocals; $\frac{8}{3} \times \frac{9}{2} \neq 1$

7. $\frac{10}{9}; 3\frac{1}{9}$ **8.** $\frac{6}{59}; \frac{26}{59}$ **9.** $\frac{5}{32}; \frac{35}{288}$ **10.** $6\frac{3}{5}$

11. $9\frac{1}{2}$ **12.** $\frac{39}{88}$ **13.** $1\frac{19}{60}$ **14.** $\frac{12}{91}$ **15.** $\frac{3}{8}$

16. $3\frac{5}{9}$ **17.** $2\frac{6}{17}$ **18.** $1\frac{1}{3}$ **19.** $16\frac{8}{9}$; You can display 16 golf balls. **20.** $4\frac{6}{7}$ hours

Practice B

1. $3\frac{3}{7} \div \frac{4}{7}$ **2.** 3 **3.** 58 **4.** $1\frac{5}{7}$ **5.** $8\frac{41}{65}$

6. $\frac{1}{12}$ **7.** $\frac{5}{6}$ **8.** $1\frac{11}{41}$ **9.** $1\frac{25}{27}$ **10.** $1\frac{47}{58}$

11. 6 holes; Multiplication **12.** $3\frac{17}{20}$ pounds; Addition **13.** $21\frac{1}{3}$ minutes; Multiplication

14. $7\frac{1}{2}$ times; Division **15.** 4 **16.** 4 **17.** 11

Practice C

1. 5 **2.** $13\frac{4}{11}$ **3.** $2\frac{5}{24}$ **4.** $6\frac{5}{6}$ **5.** $\frac{8}{39}$ **6.** $3\frac{1}{23}$

7. $4\frac{1}{8}$ **8.** $3\frac{12}{91}$ **9.** $3\frac{1}{14}$ **10.** $\frac{59}{520}$ liters

11. $6\frac{23}{27}$; You can fit 6 books. **12.** $21\frac{1}{3}$ **13.** 5

14. $1\frac{1}{12}$ **15.** $40 \div 1\frac{1}{3}$ **16.** $40 \div 1$; 40

17. 30 studs **18.** $\frac{18}{25}$ **19.** $9\frac{1}{6}$ **20.** $\frac{2}{5}$

Study Guide

1. 22 **2.** $\frac{15}{4}$ or $3\frac{3}{4}$ **3.** $\frac{7}{2}$ or $3\frac{1}{2}$ **4.** 10 **5.** $\frac{3}{5}$

6. $\frac{3}{4}$ **7.** $\frac{1}{2}$ **8.** $\frac{4}{3}$ or $1\frac{1}{3}$ **9.** $\frac{9}{5}$ **10.** $\frac{32}{11}$

11. $\frac{8}{7}$ or $1\frac{1}{7}$ **12.** $\frac{9}{8}$ or $1\frac{1}{8}$ **13.** $\frac{3}{4}$ **14.** $\frac{18}{5}$ or $3\frac{3}{5}$

15. $\frac{13}{10}$ or $1\frac{3}{10}$ **16.** $\frac{11}{6}$ or $1\frac{5}{6}$ **17.** 6 **18.** $\frac{5}{8}$ cup

Real-World Problem Solving

1. 100 lots; $33\frac{1}{3}$ lots; $28\frac{4}{7}$ lots **2.** $5000

3. $12,500

Lesson 7.5 *continued*

Challenge Practice

1. 5

2.

Men	Women
$25\frac{7}{24}$ ft	$19\frac{9}{16}$ ft
$23\frac{7}{16}$ ft	$18\frac{13}{16}$ ft
$22\frac{1}{8}$ ft	$18\frac{31}{48}$ ft
$21\frac{35}{48}$ ft	$18\frac{13}{24}$ ft
$21\frac{1}{2}$ ft	$18\frac{1}{4}$ ft

3. $22\frac{49}{60}$ ft **4.** $18\frac{61}{80}$ ft

Lesson 7.6

Practice A

1. ounces **2.** cups **3.** gallons **4.** tons
5. fluid ounces **6.** gallons **7.** pints
8. fluid ounces **9.** capacity **10.** length
11. weight **12.** capacity **13.** capacity
14. length **15.** 8 **16.** 4 **17.** 3 **18.** 20
19. 2 **20.** 32 **21.** B **22.** D **23.** cups
24. tons **25.** 16 oz

Practice B

1. tons **2.** pints **3.** fluid ounces **4.** ounces
5. pounds **6.** gallons **7.** gallon
8. fluid ounces **9.** pint **10.** cups
11. length **12.** capacity **13.** weight
14. capacity **15.** length **16.** weight **17.** 16
18. 1 **19.** 8 **20.** 8 **21.** 4 **22.** 8 **23.** C
24. B **25.** C **26.** 4 fluid ounces

Practice C

1. ounces **2.** gallons **3.** fluid ounces
4. ounces **5.** tons **6.** gallons **7.** A **8.** D
9. weight **10.** length **11.** capacity
12. weight **13.** capacity **14.** capacity **15.** 3
16. 40 **17.** 4 **18.** 6000 **19.** 4; 8; 16
20. 8; 2 **21.** pounds **22.** tons **23.** ounces
24. ounces **25.** Aluminum is very light so it
will have a large volume and steel is very heavy so
it will have a small volume. **26.** more than a
pint

27. about a pint **28.** more than a pint
29. more than a pint **30.** less than a pint
31. about a pint

Study Guide

1. pound or ounce **2.** ton **3.** ounce **4.** pint,
cup, or fluid ounce **5.** gallon **6.** fluid ounce
7. pound **8.** gallon **9.** ounce

Challenge Practice

1. a human heart **2.** a tablespoon
3. a washing machine **4.** an elephant
5. a pickup truck

Lesson 7.7

Practice A

1. 1760 **2.** 1 **3.** 4 **4.** 16 **5.** 8 **6.** 36
7. 6400 **8.** 5428 **9.** 3 **10.** 1; 144; 5
11. 2 **12.** 4 **13.** 4000 pounds **14.** 4 miles
15. 6 cups **16.** 64 ounces **17.** $2\frac{2}{3}$ feet
18. $10\frac{1}{4}$ gallons **19.** 3 quarts **20.** $1\frac{1}{4}$ tons
21. $4\frac{3}{4}$ quarts **22.** 13 lb 3 oz **23.** 6 gal 1 qt
24. 3 mi 197 feet **25.** 3 T 1974 lb
26. 1 qt 1 pt **27.** 1 ft 8 in.
28. No, the company has 2 T of extra materials.
29. $3\frac{1}{3}$ yards by 4 yards **30.** 5 pints

Practice B

1. C **2.** A **3.** F **4.** B **5.** E **6.** D
7. 2850 **8.** 1 **9.** 5499 **10.** 1; 216; 7
11. 1 **12.** 6 **13.** 10,000 pounds
14. 15,840 feet **15.** 2 cups **16.** 3 pounds
17. $1\frac{7}{12}$ feet **18.** $6\frac{3}{4}$ gallons
19. 18 fluid ounces **20.** 54 ounces
21. 64 inches **22.** 8 lb 10 oz **23.** 13 gal
24. 7 mi 960 ft **25.** 1553 lb **26.** 1 qt 1 pt
27. 5 ft 7 in. **28.** 2 quarts **29.** 432 inches
30. 28 pints **31.** 46,112 yards; 138,336 feet;
1,660,032 inches

Lesson 7.7 *continued*

Practice C

1. C   2. B   3. A   4. 6712   5. 3   6. 3462
7. 6; 24   8. 3   9. 12   10. 12,000 pounds
11. 7920 feet   12. 3 cups   13. 5 pounds
14. $19\frac{5}{12}$ feet   15. $7\frac{3}{4}$ gallons
16. 27 fluid ounces   17. 44 ounces
18. 92 inches   19. 6 lb 9 oz   20. 11 gal 2 qt
21. 8 mi 712 ft   22. 2 T 1565 lb   23. 1 pt
24. 5 ft 6 in.   25. 4 quarts   26. 216 inches
27. 18 pints   28. 2 feet; $\frac{2}{3}$ yard; $\frac{1}{2640}$ mile

Study Guide

1. 7   2. 5680   3. 151   4. $4\frac{1}{2}$ 5. $1\frac{1}{4}$ 6. $1\frac{2}{3}$
7. $2\frac{1}{2}$ ft   8. $3\frac{1}{2}$ pt   9. $2\frac{1}{4}$ c   10. 156   11. 26
12. 14 pt   13. 3 yd 2 ft   14. 10 qt

Real-World Problem Solving

1. $108\frac{1}{3}$ yards of edging, $4\frac{2}{3}$ yards of bushes
2. $140\frac{2}{3}$ yards of edging, 3 yards of bushes
3. $129\frac{1}{3}$ yards of edging, $5\frac{1}{3}$ yards of bushes
4. $133\frac{1}{3}$ yards of edging, $6\frac{2}{3}$ yards of bushes
5. $125\frac{1}{3}$ yards of edging, $3\frac{2}{3}$ yards of bushes

Challenge Practice

1. 49 cups   2. 2:40 P.M.   3. 1 cup
4. $.02; $.04; 2-liter bottle   5. 5 oz
6. 95 ft/sec

Review and Projects

Chapter Review Games and Activities

A	B	C	D
2	2	2	7
$8\frac{1}{3}$	$2\frac{1}{2}$	$4\frac{1}{2}$	$3\frac{1}{2}$
$\frac{5}{42}$	$\frac{4}{35}$	$\frac{9}{20}$	$\frac{10}{27}$
$\frac{3}{4}$	$\frac{2}{7}$	$\frac{4}{5}$	$\frac{3}{7}$
$\frac{1}{8}$	$\frac{1}{16}$	$\frac{1}{27}$	$\frac{1}{5}$
$6\frac{3}{4}$	$11\frac{1}{3}$	$13\frac{1}{5}$	$13\frac{1}{3}$
$3\frac{24}{35}$	$2\frac{2}{5}$	$\frac{13}{36}$	$1\frac{1}{6}$

A	B	C	D
5	$13\frac{3}{4}$	$4\frac{1}{2}$	$13\frac{4}{5}$
$2\frac{2}{3}$	$1\frac{1}{8}$	$2\frac{2}{5}$	$\frac{12}{35}$
$\frac{4}{21}$	$\frac{1}{15}$	$\frac{1}{6}$	$\frac{5}{36}$
$4\frac{1}{5}$	12	$7\frac{31}{35}$	$8\frac{1}{3}$
$\frac{31}{40}$	$\frac{39}{40}$	$\frac{43}{45}$	$2\frac{1}{5}$
$1\frac{17}{18}$	$2\frac{28}{33}$	$2\frac{4}{45}$	$\frac{104}{123}$

Real-Life Project

1.

Continuation of C Major Scale			
Note	C	D	E	F
Frequency	528 Hz	594 Hz	660 Hz	704 Hz

Continuation of C Major Scale			
Note	G	A	B	C
Frequency	792 Hz	880 Hz	990 Hz	1056 Hz

2.

G Major Scale			
Note	G	A	B	C
Frequency	396 Hz	445.5 Hz	495 Hz	528 Hz

G Major Scale			
Note	D	E	F	G
Frequency	594 Hz	660 Hz	742.5 Hz	792 Hz

3. A at 445.5 Hz and F at 742.5 Hz; F at 742.5 Hz is a sharp.

4. Check the student's scale to see that the notes are correctly named and the frequencies are correctly calculated.

5. Check to see that the student correctly identifies the sharps and flats from his or her scale from Question 4.

Cooperative Project

Check that students correctly calculate their sums, differences, products, and quotients and identify which of these is closest to 1.

Review and Projects *continued*

Independent Extra Credit Project

1.

Ingredient	Quantity	Capacity
Flour	5-lb bag	$17\frac{1}{2}$ cups
Sugar	5-lb bag	$11\frac{1}{4}$ cups
Salt	3-lb box	94 tablespoons
Butter	$\frac{1}{2}$-lb tub	16 tablespoons
Baking Powder	7-oz can	42 teaspoons
Baking Soda	16-oz box	96 teaspoons

2. Check to see that the student finds an appropriate recipe with the serving size and finds the correct number of batches so every person in the class can have at least one serving.

3. Check to see that the correct amount of each ingredient is calculated according to the number of batches.

4. Check to see that the correct number of bags, containers, boxes, etc. that need to be purchased is determined for each ingredient.

5. Check to see that the correct number of containers that need to be purchased is determined for each wet ingredient, where possible.

Cumulative Practice

1. 20 **2.** 13 **3.** 2 **4.** 5.9 cm **5.** 4.3 cm
6. $6\frac{7}{12}$ h **7.** About $11\frac{1}{4}$ hours **8.** 35 **9.** 345
10. 3.64 **11.** 10.85 **12.** 2.946 **13.** $0.82\overline{4}$
14. 0.0502 **15.** 212.5 **16.** $\frac{5}{8}$ **17.** 1 **18.** $\frac{7}{8}$
19. $\frac{1}{8}$ **20.** $8\frac{5}{7}$ **21.** $2\frac{3}{8}$ **22.** $2\frac{2}{3}$ **23.** $3\frac{7}{10}$
24. 1.024, 1.12, 1.21 **25.** 0.68, 0.7, 0.71
26. $\frac{8}{15}, \frac{11}{15}, \frac{13}{15}$ **27.** $\frac{1}{9}, \frac{1}{7}, \frac{1}{6}$ **28.** 57 **29.** 54
30. 185 **31.** 168 **32.** 3.02 **33.** 10.4
34. 7.6 **35.** 200 **36.** 0.525 **37.** 2, 3, 6
38. 3, 5 **39.** 3, 5, 9 **40.** 2, 5, 10 **41.** 12; 24
42. 6; 120 **43.** 7; 70 **44.** 6; 252 **45.** 36
46. 13 **47.** 2 **48.** 38 **49.** 4 h 10 min
50. 3 h 20 min **51.** 2 h 40 min **52.** $1\frac{1}{3}$
53. $\frac{15}{16}$ **54.** $\frac{8}{21}$ **55.** $\frac{3}{16}$ **56.** $1\frac{31}{32}$ **57.** $5\frac{5}{6}$
58. $1\frac{1}{6}$ **59.** 42 **60.** 9 **61.** $1\frac{4}{5}$ **62.** $19\frac{1}{2}$
63. $12\frac{3}{4}$